Copyright © 2020 Stella Mar Films

*Published by Stella Mar Films LLC | Catholic Shop LLC | Queen of Peace Productions*

All rights reserved. No part of this book maybe used or reproduced in any manner whatsoever without the written permission of the Publisher.

**iMedjugorje: Volume 1** (2019-2020) | *Softcover Edition*

ISBN: 978-0-9978906-8-6

Printed and bound in the United States of America.
*Purchase additional copies and contact the publisher online at iMedjugorje.com, StellaMar.org, and/or CatholicShop.com.*

# The iMedjugorje Story

One of the best parts about traveling to Medjugorje—whether we're working on a new film or leading a group of pilgrims—is the people we meet.

Every pilgrim has a story to tell, and pilgrims are the heart of Medjugorje. They often become transmitters of Our Lady's messages when they return home, and their testimonies bring Medjugorje to all parts of the world.

One of our missions has been to document pilgrim testimonies and present them as evidence of the abundant miracles and graces that people find in Medjugorje. And so—with incredible support from the **Apostles of Love** community *(www.Patreon.com/Apostles)* —our team at *Stella Mar Films* & *Queen of Peace Productions* created *iMedjugorje.com* to share these powerful stories with the rest of the world.

Now we're excited to bring you this book— a collection of stories from the first year of iMedjugorje—and we hope to continue capturing as many Medjugorje testimonies as we can in the coming years.

Please keep our work in your prayers, and thank you for being an Apostle of Love!

~*Cimela, Jessi, & Sean*

# The Collaborators

**Jozo Ivankovic** and his father, **Damir**, run Foto Video Studio DANI, the video production studio in Medjugorje. As strong believers in the apparitions, they've been a huge help for us in our work there. We're grateful for their friendship and constant support.

Jozo Ivankovic is also an Associate Producer for our film *Where There is Darkness*. We had the honor of hosting his first visit to the United States, and he brought with him his expert drone flying skills.

As part of our Medjugorje Internship program, **Emily Black** from Dalmally, Scotland helped us launch iMedjugorje and capture some of the first iMedjugorje stories. She also spent time working in our studio in Florida as an Associate Producer of *Where There is Darkness*.

"Three days after submitting my Honours dissertation, I was on a flight to Orlando. I'd never left Europe before and I felt a little daunted… Their passion for their craft and their enthusiasm for sharing Fateher Rene's story was infectious."     ~Emily Black

**Jarred Hicks,** our second Medjugorje intern, is from sunny California. He lived in Medjugorje for two months during the summer of 2019. He is a recent graduate of Franciscan University.

"In 2017, while studying abroad in Gaming, Austria, I went on a weekend trip to Medjugorje. I was honored to serve alongside the team at Stella Mar Films! These are incredible individuals with hearts of gold doing this work."   ~Jarred Hicks

This is my first time here in Medjugorje. We're a parish from East London and there are ten of us here. We all just decided as a group to come out—we had our calling.

It's been great to hear stories about the apparitions. Climbing up Apparition Hill yesterday was difficult. I had the rosary in hand because getting to the first mystery I was like, 'we're not going to be able to do this, it's too slippery.'

But it was fantastic, we got up and down safely. A member of the group who wasn't able to get up when he came before followed us. Even though he walks with a stick, he was able to make it. It's a special place and I'm looking forward to the rest of our time here.

~Ben, London UK

I think all of us, in a way, are called by Our Lady, so I felt sort of called to come. But I also think it's for renewal. I just discerned out of the Society of Jesus [the Jesuit Order] and it's an emotional thing doing that because you kind of question do I have a vocation? And so I sort of just needed to recharge my batteries. And I've used the time as a Lenten retreat to grow closer to God. I spent time getting to know Him, letting the love grow between us, and then I feel like from that I'll be able to make a decision to continue applying to the diocese [...]

I remember Archbishop Hoser was talking about how when you enter into Medjugorje, it's sort of like entering into a spiritual dimension. And it's really true. There's such special grace here. It really touches your heart. He said it the best, you enter into the spiritual dimension, it sort of transforms you and renews you and gives you insight into God's plan for you.

It's a really special place, but it can be emotionally exhausting too. Because so many powerful things hit you at once.

~Michael, USA

**Molly:** We just met four days ago. We came as a group but I didn't know anybody and I'd never been here before. It's just been the most amazing, wonderful, joyful, loving experience. I don't want to leave.

**Paula:** We're leaving today and we've all been crying. We don't want to leave Our Lady and Jesus. I was here in 1989 and it was so profound for me, and so it is thirty years later that I got to return to Medjugorje. I'm finding it just as powerful and peaceful and beautiful as before. In '89 I wanted to come so bad that I came by myself with no plans, but Our Lady took care of me — found me a place to stay, found me people.

**Molly:** And in a long, roundabout way, that's how we all ended up here.

**Paula:** Yeah! My grandmother told me, then I told my friend David, and David arranged a group from his church – so now we're all here!

I'm here on pilgrimage with my school. We're all sixteen/seventeen. It is just amazing, so different. It's such a special place. It's my first time here, and I really love it. We didn't know what to expect, didn't know what we'd be doing every day. We knew we were going to mass, but not twice a day. If we were told to go to mass twice a day at home, we would be like 'oh my gosh, I'm not going.' But here it's just different and mass is so nice.

~*Gráinne, Ireland*

We're on a school trip from Donegal in Ireland. It's our first time here. We've been here two days. It's class, a great experience. It is very relaxing. The thing last night, what was it called?"

– "Adoration."

–"Yeah, that was really peaceful."

– "Aye, the adoration was good last night.

It was our first time doing it—we don't have that at home. ~*School Group, Ireland*

We're on pilgrimage from Bray in Ireland. We brought thirty students with us, that's why we're here. It's my 12th or 13th time here and we come every year with the students. They're 17 years of age, so it is the right time for them to start asking questions and really challenge themselves on how they can develop their faith and get that personal relationship with God.

I love it. It's great for them. When I get a few minutes to myself it's perfect, it's peaceful. It's what I need. But it's full on when you have thirty kids with you!

~*Seamus, Ireland*

**Evelyn:** We're both school teachers. Coming here is magical. It is very peaceful, very prayerful. We're loving it.

**Cleoma:** We teach 12-18 year olds. The students get an awful lot from it. There are lots of amazing things happening. It is very personal for the students. It's daily, each student can get something different from the experience.

**Evelyn:** We're 'medjheads' all the way!

My name is Svjetlana. I am 34 years old. I am Croatian and I was born in Bosnia. When the war started in the 1990s, my family and I moved to Herzegovina as refugees, and that is how Medjugorje became a big part of my family's life.

My parents had a huge conversion, and even though we lost everything in the war, we had Medjugorje. In 1996 we moved together as a family to Canada and I can see now how Our Lady stayed with us through the ups and downs, the trials of life. Our Lady had a plan that I didn't know at the time.

About nine years ago, my sister entered a religious community in Croatia, and we started coming back here more to visit. I never planned to live here, but I stayed a few summers in a row and I met Marija the visionary, and we became friends.

Then about three years ago, a friend of mine who is a guide inspired me to do the official guide test. I knew it was an opportunity I had to take because it was another five years until the next test. It wasn't something I had planned to do and I was thinking of moving back to Canada. I did the test and became a guide. I can really see that this is what I am meant to do—it is a calling, not a job. It is not easy, but it is very rewarding.

I always remind myself that Our Lady is the true guide; She is the one in charge. Sharing Our Lady's messages with the pilgrims, I receive so much every day.

I am thankful to God for this journey, and for Our Lady staying with me and protecting my family in so many ways.

~*Svjetlana, Medjugorje Guide*

## OUR LADY'S MESSAGE TO MIRJANA ON JANUARY 2, 2019

"Dear children, sadly, among you, my children, there is so much battle, hatred, personal interests and selfishness. My children, so easily you forget my Son, His words, His love. Faith is being extinguished in many souls, and hearts are being grasped by material things of the world.

But my motherly heart knows that there are still those who believe and love, who are seeking how to draw all the closer to my Son, who are tirelessly seeking my Son–then, in this way, they are also seeking me. These are the humble and the meek with their pain and suffering which they carry in silence with their hopes and, above all, with their faith. These are the apostles of my love.

My children, apostles of my love, I am teaching you that my Son is not only asking for continuous prayers, but also for works and feelings–that you believe, that you pray, that with your personal prayers you grow in faith, that you grow in love. To love each other is what He asks for–that is the way to eternal life.

My children, do not forget that my Son brought the light to this world, and He brought it to those who wanted to see it and receive it. You be those, because this is the light of truth, peace and love. I am leading you in a motherly way to adore my Son; that you love my Son with me; that your thoughts, words and actions may be directed to My Son–that they may be in His name. Then my heart will be fulfilled. Thank you."

~Our Lady Queen of Peace, January 2

I came in 1990 with a youth group when I was 14 years old. I saw lots of signs and had an encounter with Our Lady, and it gave me solid ground to stand on through the difficult high school and college years.

I have found that I need to give my kids an experience, an encounter with God that's outside of me and my lens and our parish. We have to get them out so that they can realize what a treasure our family prayer is and what a treasure the Eucharist is and our parish is back home. But just sitting at home, going to school and having it all just preached to them, they also need to have their own encounter. And so coming to Medjugorje, they get away and they can encounter God in a new way, just themselves and then they can come home and they realize the treasure that it is back home.

So I'm bringing the whole family this June. I have seven kids. We're gonna give them to Our Lady and let her have them for two weeks!
~Mike, Indiana USA

*iMedj Note: Mike's parents run MaryTV which shares daily events of Medjugorje*

I came here during the war in 1993 as a charity worker to help refugees. I stayed two years the first time, then I came back in 2007.

I built a house, thought it would be a holiday house but it became a permanent house. I felt Our Lady was inviting me to stay, but I didn't want to at first. Then my spiritual director said it is better to obey, so I am obeying. Like everywhere, you have to carry your cross—there is the good side and the more difficult side.

When you live here you lose the grace of the pilgrims; you're not a pilgrim anymore. You have to discover a new way of living here. The most important part is the evening program, the three hours of prayer. That is what Our Lady asked of us. That is the only reason for being here to be honest.

*~Charlie, Medjugorje*

Sixteen years ago, I started working in Medjugorje as a guide. It was just at that time when my conversion began. I say 'began' because conversion is not something from one day to another, but instead it's a process throughout your whole life.

That's why when I felt God's love and the love of our Holy Mother, the Virgin Mary, I could not resist Him. And I simply just left everything and I came to work as a guide. And so after 16 years I've realized, more than a job, this is a vocation. I thank God day after day for having called me to serve him in this way.

I believe the most special experience for the pilgrims who come is the Sacrament of Reconciliation. This is where they encounter Jesus, and encounter forgiveness and His mercy [...]

Being a part of the movie, *Mary's Land*, is one of the most beautiful experiences I've had related to Medjugorje. Although, at first, I said I didn't want to participate in the film, I felt it was vain to be in a film because I was seeing it with the eyes of the world. However, when I found out I could help someone, that it could touch someone's heart, I decided to be a part of it.

Juan Manuel [Director of the film] was talking to me about all he had planned to film for the interviews and translations. At first I was only going to help him with translation and 20 minutes later he said he wanted me to be in the film. My first response was no, but after that he asked me if I had a spiritual director and if he could talk to them. Finally, after talking with my spiritual director, I accepted to do it because my spiritual director said I should do it. So, today I thank God for that experience because it truly is a film that has touched many hearts, in a way that only the Holy Spirit can through us.

~*Filka, Medjugorje Guide*

My daughter Lucija and I have come here from Zagreb, the capital of Croatia. Medjugorje is such a special place... it is a spa for our souls. We came on pilgrimage for the first time in 2014, and since then we come

We started our pilgrimage yesterday evening when we drove 7 hours, the whole night. We arrived at 6 this morning and went immediately to climb Krizevac.

After that, we visited Cenacolo, the community for people who are dealing with different addiction problems. They are living in community, without any money, living on God's providence, working, praying, getting to know themselves, and getting to know God.

This afternoon we will go to Mass, and in the evening to Adoration. For us, Adoration is the most beautiful part of Medjugorje. It is so nice to be in the presence of our Lord in the Blessed Sacrament, together with people from different parts of the world, singing and praying to the Lord in different languages. We hope that heaven looks like that [...]

This time, we met the dear people from Stella Mar Films. It is an interesting story, how I got in contact with them. I saw this very, very beautiful documentary about Medjugorje on YouTube, it is called *The Triumph*. It is about Ben, a young American who is in Medjugorje, trying to find out if there really is a God, if Mother Mary really is coming here, and trying to deal with his addictions. I liked the movie so much that I translated it to Croatian. Even though I'm not their official translator, Stella Mar have recognized my enthusiasm and asked me to help with their other projects. Through doing this, I have found my way of contributing to spreading God's message to the world.

*It is so nice to be here, because here is our Mother. And where Mother is, there is home.*
~*Elvira with her daughter Lucija, Croatia*

## OUR LADY'S MESSAGE TO MIRJANA ON FEBRUARY 2, 2019

"Dear children, The love and goodness of the Heavenly Father give revelations which make faith grow, for it to be interpreted, that it may bring peace, certainty and hope. In this way, I, too, my children—through the merciful love of the Heavenly Father—always, anew, am showing you the way to my Son, to eternal salvation. But, unfortunately, many of my children do not want to hear me; many of my children are of two minds. And I—I always, in time and beyond time, magnified the Lord for all that He has done in me and through me.

My Son gives Himself to you and breaks the bread with you. He speaks the words of eternal life to you so that you may carry them to everyone. And you, my children, apostles of my love, what are you afraid of when my Son is with you? Offer your souls to Him so that He can be in them and that He can make you instruments of faith, instruments of love.

My children, live the Gospel, live merciful love for your neighbors, and, above all, live love for the Heavenly Father. My children, you are not united by chance. The Heavenly Father does not unite anyone by chance. My Son speaks to your souls. I speak to your heart. As a mother I am saying to you: set out with me, love one another, give witness. Do not be afraid, with your example, to defend the truth—the Word of God which is eternal and never changes. My children, whoever acts in the light of merciful love and truth is always helped by Heaven and is not alone.

Apostles of my love, may you always be recognized among all others by your hiddenness, love and radiance. I am with you. Thank you."   ~*Our Lady Queen of Peace, February 2*

The last time I was here, I got a hoarseness in my throat. Then when I got home, I got it investigated. They found a lump on my vocal cord; they took it off and it was cancerous. For about two months, I was getting ready to do therapy for 25 sessions. They put a cage on your head and bolt you to the table because you can't have any movement at all. It was just horrific.

Medjugorje helped me through all that. Because I did a routine every day for 25 sessions and I started praying for my grandchildren, just offering the whole thing up for my grandchildren Saying an Our Father, a Hail Mary, a Glory Be for Christina… and move on to the next grandchild while it was happening. It also helped me know where I was in the time period that it was taking to do it. So when I came to a certain name, I said it's just another two and then it's over. It helped praying for them and offering it up.

I just accepted the whole thing and offered it up. A few years ago, I wouldn't have been able to do that. Medjugorje has really strengthened my faith for me to do that. Thank God.

We have come 30-something times. We've lost count at this stage. Marie came first in 1986. We always went on holiday to Spain or Portugal, and all that, never the same place twice.

Always went somewhere else the next year. Then when we came to Medjugorje, I never went anywhere after that. We just keep coming to Medjugorje all the time. Twice a year, for three or four weeks. There's just something special about it. The atmosphere.

*Our Lady is appearing here. There's a natural draw. I was drawn here all the time.*

Our two grandchildren were here last week. Our oldest grandchild, that's her 7th time here and the other for her 2nd time. We have two more coming for the Youth Festival this year, that's their first time coming over.

I was coming here for a long time and still had my doubts about it because I am not one to jump into something very quick and just believe. I have to sort of investigate it and make up my own mind, then when I did, I couldn't see any way that it was false.

There's a policeman friend here and what made him believe in Medjugorje was, he said if anything happened in England, he would bring all the young lads in and he would pick on the weakest or the youngest and he would always break and tell the story, say what really happened.

When he saw [visionary] Jacov, a 10-year-old child knelt down on his knees going over to the church every night for three hours. It was impossible that they were telling lies. As a policeman, his experience was that there's always one that would break. It's impossible for 6 people to keep it up for 38 years--you would just go mad. So that's what convinced him.

~*Joe, Ireland*

I'm here on pilgrimage. This is my fifth time coming here.

I feel I need to come once a year to recharge my batteries, and it does recharge my batteries.

It's a wonderful place to be—a wonderful place.

*~Wendy, England*

I first came to Medjugorje when I was fourteen, and since then I've been coming once or twice a year.

This is my first time being here for Palm Sunday - it's been amazing! It reminds me of the Youth Festival with all the people.

There's just a huge sense of peace here. I can't describe it—it's like coming home every time.

*~Zoe, England*

**Mom:** It is a really peaceful place. People are really friendly and you feel Our Lady's presence here.

**Dad:** We decided to go to Apparition Hill and Cross Mountain yesterday. We took the children and they managed to climb both in one day!

**Mom:** It was a special grace.

*~The Fernandes Family*

Wherever I go, he goes and vice versa.

We were able to join Guy Murphy [Totally Yours Pilgrimages] in the Holy Land last year. And then from the Holy Land it's just like the story of the Bible popping up in front of your eyes. So everything is more intimate when you read scriptures.

You go on pilgrimage, you come back home a different person. There's always going to be conversion. It's not going to be obvious. It's a journey. So when you journey you're going to have changes, and then from there you're going to polish it. It's not going to be perfect but you're going to get better.

Coming with my husband is different. At least we're on the same page, because each individual, even if you're siblings or any kind of relationship, there's always going to be different levels of where you are in your spiritual life. But we're helping each other.

Praying the Rosary — we've been praying together as much as we can. Before, I would be like, "Come on. Be attentive." Now when we're praying, he will be the one waking me up. He's like, "Come on. You're sleeping. You shouldn't be sleeping." It helped our spiritual growth.

He was like, "Okay go wherever you want to go because I've been hearing Medjugorje from you." So as we prepared, I started reading. And then I started fasting. And I was like, "Man this one is hard." But it's not going to happen overnight. There's always going to be steps.

~*Barbara and her husband Sonny, USA*

## OUR LADY'S MESSAGE TO MIRJANA ON MARCH 2, 2019

"Dear children, I call you 'apostles of my love'. I am showing you my Son who is the true peace and the true love. As a mother, through the mercy of God, I desire to lead you to Him.

My children, this is why I am calling you to reflect on yourselves, starting out from my Son, that you look to Him with the heart and that you may see with the heart where you are and where your life is going.

My children, I am calling you to comprehend that it is, thanks to my Son, that you live– through His love and sacrifice. You are asking of my Son to be merciful to you and I am calling you to mercy.

You are asking of Him to be good to you and to forgive you, and for how long am I imploring you, my children, to for-give and to love all the people whom you meet? When you comprehend my words with the heart, you will compre-hend and come to know the true love and you will be able to be apostles of that love, my apostles, my dear children. Thank you."

~Our Lady Queen of Peace, March 2

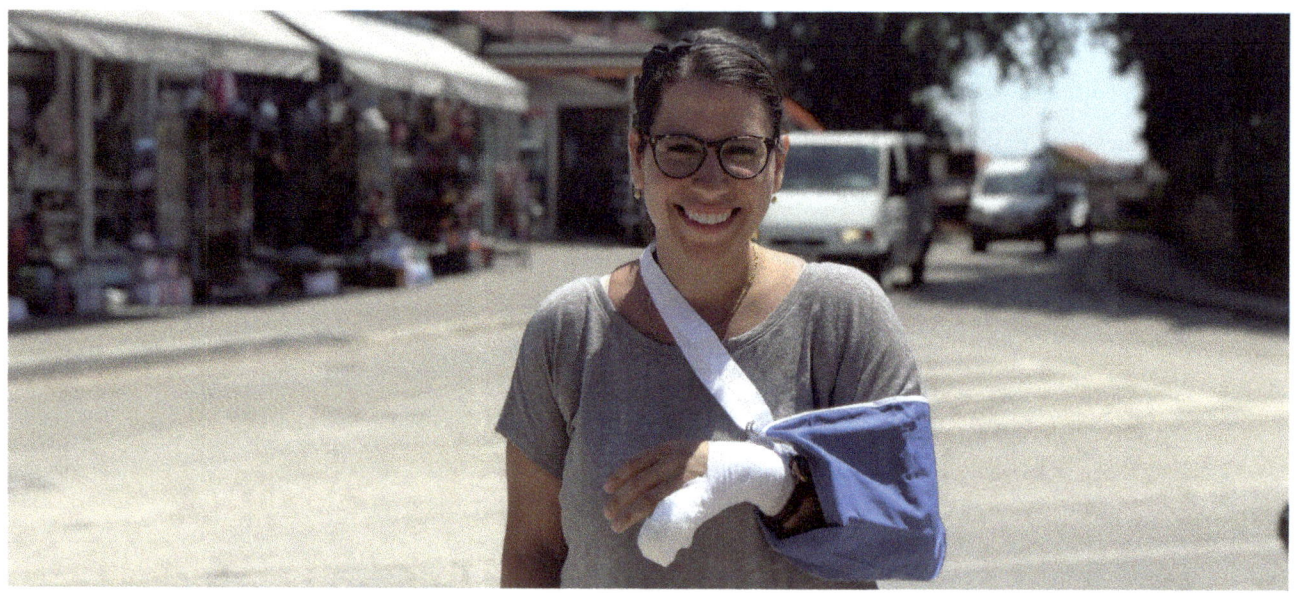

I had only been in Medjugorje for 12 hours when I faced an unexpected situation. Long story short, my finger got slammed in a door and I had to be taken to the emergency room in Mostar. Turns out I actually lost some of my finger flesh and had to have my bone shaved down in order to have my finger stitched up.

At the time it was just crazy. Nothing was registering because things escalated so quickly. I do believe that through it all Our Blessed Mother gave me the graces to endure the shock and pain, which I think is how it always happens in life with Our Blessed Mother.

I know when you are in a lot of suffering and pain you can offer it up. Usually I don't have a lot of physical pain, suffering we all have, so immediately when it happened, I was like "Oh my gosh I have so many things I have to offer this up for." As it continues to hurt, I continue to offer it up for people, their conversions, and various situations... and my future husband.

Of all the places this could have happened, I love that it happened in Medjugorje. It feels more meaningful and I've been asking myself what it is that I am supposed to learn from this freak accident, but only time will tell. Before I always felt as though I had left a part of my heart in Medjugorje, now I've left part of my finger there too.

~*Melissa, Texas USA*

My parish is called Kaduha. It's 35 kilometers away from Kibeho. Medjugorje and Kibeho have so many similarities. It was the same year that the Blessed Mother appeared in Kibeho and here. Here, it was June 24th. Kibeho was November 28th, 1981.

Another similarity is the messages. Mary comes here and says pray; convert. Kibeho is the same— pray with a sincere heart. Here, pray from the heart. So that is the same.

She says she is the Queen of Peace here. And even Kibeho said convert and leave your ways, you need peace among yourselves. And she connected it with, if you don't change your heart, you don't change your lives, bad things will happen to the country. And it was a prediction of genocide that took place in '94 in Rwanda. Terrible. 100 days; 1 million people massacred. And you know, here also the Serbs massacred over 100,000.

The messages just say it in a different way, but they are the same— fundamentally the same. She is calling all of us to convert; to pray with sincerity of heart; to search for peace between us and God. And if there is no peace between us and God, definitely there is no peace between man and man. That is where you get hatred, revenge, killing, genocide— it comes from those who lack peace.  ~*Fr. Bernard, Uganda*

I was a first-year nursing student, and my friend that I'd met, her godmother came here. So after that, there was big news about Medjugorje — you've got to come; this place is wonderful. I'd never been anywhere. Homebird. And I thought, 'I'm not going.'

So what happens is, they book my ticket without me knowing. I had no way out. I had to come. That was October 1984. And I was here for four days.

At first, I didn't think very much of the place. I did the whole walk around from Krizevac to Podbrodo around to the church again, praying the Rosary. And then I went to the evening mass.

I just think that there was a grace. Like a silent grace that you can't touch, but just having your soul present in that church of St. James, that then God can do what He wants with you. And that's how I ended up here. What happened was, this friend of mine, she was cleaning the church. Everybody was going out. And I thought, do the good deed and help her brush up, you know, in between the pews. So I was doing that and there was one man left with black hair like Elvis. So I told him, 'Get out of the pew because I need to sweep.' And my heart was going bump-a-dee-bump-a-dee-bump.

I went back to England and came again, and I bumped into him again. And then I realized he's in the prayer group. And because he was in the prayer group, they had a four-year commitment not to choose a wife, not to choose a vocation, just to have these three hours of prayer and Our Lady guide it. So he showed absolutely no interest in me. I nearly died.

We knew each other, but we weren't romantically attached. My heart was taken the very first time I saw him. And then he admitted to me after we got married, that his was too.

But then we just prayed. We could pray in the same language, but we couldn't speak in the same language. And then when we got married, we still couldn't speak to each other in the same language. But the connection was, I thought I saw great integrity and great devotion. I could've been wrong, but thank God I was right. He then learned English after the first year of us being married.
~Rosie, Medjugorje

*iMedj Note: Rosie is the host of Tea with Rosie/Mary TV.*

## OUR LADY'S MESSAGE TO MIRJANA ON MARCH 18, 2019

"My children—As a mother, as the Queen of Peace, I am calling you to accept my Son so that He can grant you peace of soul—that He can grant you that which is just, which is good for you.

My children, my Son knows you. He lived the life of man, and at the same time of God: a wondrous life—human flesh, divine Spirit.

Therefore, my children, while my Son is looking at you with His eyes of God, He penetrates into your hearts. His tender, warm eyes are looking for Himself in your heart. My Children, can He find Himself [there]?

Accept Him, and then the moments of pain and suffering will become moments of tenderness.

Accept Him, and you will have peace in [your] soul—you will spread it to all those around you—and this is what you now need the most. Heed me, my children. Pray for the shepherds, for those whose hands my Son has blessed. Thank you."

~Our Lady Queen of Peace, March 18

I am Father Diego Gonzalez, from the Messengers of Peace Community in Argentina. I am Colombian, and for 10 years, beginning when I started my formation in the seminary, I have accompanied the Latin pilgrims to Medjugorje.

We have been here for five days and have visited Apparition Hill, Cross Mountain and we are headed to where Our Lady gives her messages. It's a path of prayer— we offer up our sufferings— and a place of interior healing. We have had the blessing to spend time with the visionary Mirjana and her husband and hear her testimony as we are staying with her.

We purposefully chose this time, before the apparition, to come so that we can prepare the hearts of the pilgrims so that when the day of the apparition comes, they can truly receive the blessings that our God wants to pour out over us through the apparitions of the Virgin Mary.

Mary brings us to Jesus. She wants us to put Jesus first in our lives. To me, this is a very big blessing. I always say that Medjugorge is a place overflowing with prayer, which tells you this is a place where Our Lady has appeared. She has been giving the grace of faith to this place since even before the apparitions.

And She herself asked the town to pray and it's a town that is very faithful. It's a very special place where one comes. You find out that what you thought were assurances of your beliefs are not God. You fall to pieces and you feel your heart break but it's okay because this is your Mother's house— the place where you cry and where you break down.

Once you break down, you realize that it was fake reassurances and this is when you can really begin to construct something new in your life, in the presence of God, taken by the hand of Jesus and Mary to carry you forward.

That's why for me every time I come here, I get the graces from God to continue to grow in this path of sanctity. And also, it's great as a priest to hear all the peoples' confessions. It's truly a conversion of the heart.

~ *Fr. Diego Gonzalez, Argentina*

*"I always say that Medjugorge is a place overflowing with prayer, which tells you this is a place where Our Lady has appeared."* -Fr. Diego Gonzalez

## OUR LADY'S MESSAGE TO MIRJANA ON APRIL 2, 2019

"Dear children, as a mother who knows her children, I know that you are crying out for my Son. I know that you are crying out for truth, for peace, for that which is pure and not deceptive.

That is why I, as a mother, through the love of God, am addressing you and calling you, that by prayer and a pure and open heart within yourselves, you may come to know my Son– His love, His merciful heart.

My Son saw beauty in all things. He seeks the good in all souls—even that which is little and hidden—so as to forgive evil.

Therefore, my children, apostles of my love, I am calling you to adore Him, to ceaselessly give Him thanks, and to be worthy. Because He has spoken to you divine words, the words of God, the words which are for all and forever.

Therefore, my children, live joy, radiance, unity and mutual love. This is what you need in today's world. In this way you will be apostles of my love. In this way you will witness my Son in the right way. Thank you."

~Our Lady Queen of Peace, April 2

My wife and I were trying to have a kid, and we weren't having any luck. We were going to the doctor, but nobody knew. My wife is very private. I have a great devotion to Our Lady of Lourdes. So I said, "Let's say a novena to Our Lady of Lourdes to have a baby."

In nine days, we said the novena. The morning of the tenth day, my wife's best girlfriend's husband, who is a lawyer, called us. He knew nothing about our situation.

He said, "We have a little baby boy that needs to be adopted, and they want him to go to a good, Catholic family, and we thought about you two. Would you adopt this baby? The only problem is, he's three months early. He's 1lb 15oz."

So I said, "Sure, we'll take him."

And then a year later, they call again, the mother was pregnant again. Would we take that baby? And so that was our son, Rafael.

So we got two babies for one novena.

A year ago, last April, my oldest son Damian's liver shut down. He was in Wisconsin where he lives with his wife. He was gonna die. So we rushed up there.

We had tons of prayers, convents of nuns praying for him, tons of Lourdes water. Now, he keeps saying, "The doctors saved me."

The doctors, they were amazed. They were like, "His liver just jumped back." While he was in the hospital, he was holding onto the rosary, praying and all that stuff. Once he got out, he went back to being cynical.

He kept saying, "Well, Dad, you get all the signs. I don't have any signs." I said, "Damian, the way you were born was your sign." "No, I want my own sign."

So I started praying for Mary's intercession that she would manifest herself to Damian in a special way and that he would know the love of Jesus for him. That was my prayer, every day, all last year. Well, three months ago, I was at the altar at Mass during the consecration, and I get this message. And the message was, "Damian needs to go to Medjugorje for Mary to manifest herself." I said, "Okay God, you're gonna have to make it happen because I don't have the money." So I just kept praying.

And then three weeks later, I'm at Mass, and I said the same prayer again. Then Marilyn comes up to me, who knows nothing about Damian, and she said, "Something's been on my heart for months now, but I'm able to tell you today." And I said, "What?" She said, "I'm sending you to Medjugorje. Free." So I told Damian, and he's here. And he's getting signs.

I said, "God wants you to accept the truth. You have so many gifts. Once you accept the Lord, you will be a great evangelizer. And you will go out there, and you can help people." And I told him about Catherine of Siena who was so bold she told the pope, "Get out of Avignon. Get back to Rome. That's what God's telling me. You're hurting the church." That was the pope! And she was just a lay person. I always thought she was a nun. She wasn't a nun. I said, "You have that leadership power to challenge with respect.

~*Deacon Ed, Iowa USA*

For more than 30 years, I am coming to Medjugorje. When Mother started appearing in Medjugorje, I was making jokes. I was a "vagabundo." A sailor. My life was "estronado"– it was crazy. For me nothing was important, except women. Nothing else. Only women. I went to war, and faced tragedy. That was part of the transformation in my life. I couldn't move. All my friends were gone. Only God was by me, and Mother. That was the beginning of my path to God.

Back at that time I visited the Community Cenacolo. Many times, I was there. During these days, Mirjana would experience her 2nd of the month apparitions there.

*iMedj Note: In 2009, the 2nd of the month apparitions took place at the Blue Cross, the base of Apparition Hill.*

It was a confusing time at first. Where? Who? It was just me and a few others helping. I had some experience [when the apparitions took place in] Cenacolo. Only God knows and Mother know why I am there. I am the only one that is not from the village. It's not my wish, or my choice. God knows much better than me. How many pilgrims come in the cold, warm, winds. So many! Traveling here from all over the world. It is so hard. There are so many pilgrims. They want in. They are screaming to be close to Mirjana but the section is reserved for priests, the sick, etc.

I get there around half past 4AM or before. I close the place in, because so many want to come in. They don't care. I am tired. The same situation only different people. Always the same situation. Everybody wants in. Some making trouble. Mirjana knows why I am there. I think she is proud. 11 years doing this but I am tired. Many times I thought I would stop. This is the program of God. But all is possible for God, and Mother. Thanks to them. They know why I am there. And I don't want to know why. Thanks to them.

*iMedj Note: While interviewing Mate a pilgrim approached with a question.*

**Italian Pilgrim:** Tomorrow morning, at what time is the apparition?

**Mate:** Listen, come there, and wait and pray. Mirjana will come around 20 minutes past 8 AM. When Mother comes, we have to wait. Pray and wait.

**Italian Pilgrim:** I would like to stay closer to Mirjana. If we go around 6AM in the morning hopefully we can be…

**Mate:** Don't look where you are, stand somewhere in the peace. What do you want to see? You can be in the peace. Peace in the heart, not in the brain. If you have stone in your heart, there's no place for love and peace. Tomorrow in the morning pray for this stone to leave.

*~Mate, Croatia*

## OUR LADY'S MESSAGE TO MIRJANA ON MAY 2, 2019

"Dear children, with a motherly love I am calling you to respond to the great love of my Son, with pure and open hearts, with complete trust. I know the greatness of His love. I carried Him within me, the Host in the heart, the light and the love of the world.

My children, also my addressing you is a sign of the love and tenderness of the Heavenly Father—a big smile filled with the love of my Son, a call to eternal life.

Out of love, the Blood of my Son was shed for you. That Precious Blood is for your salvation, for eternal life. The Heavenly Father created man for eternal happiness. It is not possible—for you who know the love of my Son and who follow Him—to die. Life triumphed; my Son is alive.

Therefore, my children, apostles of my love, may prayer show you the way and the means of spreading the love of my Son—prayer in the most exalted form.

My children, also when you strive to live the words of my Son, you are praying. When you love the people whom you meet, you are spreading the love of my Son. It is love that opens the doors of Paradise.

My children, from the beginning, I prayed for the Church. Therefore, I am also calling you, apostles of my love, to pray for the Church and her servants—for those whom my Son called. Thank you."  ~Our Lady Queen of Peace, May 2

I've been here over one month now. It's the longest I've ever been out here. It's a real blessing that I am actually out here.

I've been coming to Medjugorje all my life, partly for Mary's Meals and my dad's work there, and also on pilgrimages, especially to the Youth Festival. I've been to 6 of the last 7. It's been a massive part of my life always.

I'm here working with Mary's Meals and working with pilgrims all day. People come in and want to find out more about Mary's Meals, we give them information, as well as people come to fast on Wednesdays and Fridays. We give them free fasting bread and water and also often have conversations about prayer and Medjugorje.

I'm studying primary teaching. I just finished my first year and when I go back in September, I go back to start studying again. I think it's been an amazing chance for me to get into a better routine in terms of my prayer life and it's definitely that I will try to take away and implement into my own life. Make sure I get my priorities straight with faith first.

*The youth festival is absolutely amazing, it can be truly life changing. I think it's so inspiring to be among so many young Catholics from all of over the world.*

I don't think there's another place where you can get that sort of experience and that kind of motivation – feeling of belonging in the faith and remember that being Catholic is normal and how we should be. Just seeing that you can have a good, normal, fun life and still be Catholics well. I think it's a really good place to realize that.

~Ben, Scotland

**Mary:** This is my third time here. The first time I came I was in high school. He didn't know anything about Medjugorje before he met me. I've been telling him about it and trying to get him to come for the last, I don't know how many years.

**Matt:** Three.

**Mary:** We've been married for like three and a half years. Finally, in November, I convinced him to come this time. It's nice that he finally gets to experience it for himself instead of just hearing me talk about it because he would be like, "I don't get it. What is it?" And I was like, "I don't know. There's just something about the place. You just have to go there and experience it yourself." So then he finally did. I'm really happy that he finally came.

**Matt:** I'm one who appreciates natural beauty, and this place is just beautiful. Just gorgeous. I love the mountains. Even though it's been raining, that's been kind of nice too.

One of my favorite experiences was meeting the people. Our group is really awesome; everybody here, like Miki and Mirjana.

*Everybody just seems genuine and happy and sincere. I think that is probably the most powerful for me.*

*~Mary and Matt, USA*

I don't know what the next step in my life is so I'm very open to whatever God wants that to be. But my allegory is, I'm climbing Cross Mountain and it's wet and all I can think about is my next step.

And that's what I think God is saying. Don't worry about what's over there. Safely make the next step.

*It is my first time here. And I did feel called to be here.*

I'm in a Carmelite parish up in western Washington. I get a call from church. They said, "Hey, I've got something here for you. Somebody left you something. Come and get it." And I'm like, "That sounds weird but okay. Whatever." So I show up. And I can tell it's a book but it's really cool because it's wrapped in the Sunday comics.

And it's the book The Message by Wayne Weible. And this gal I barely know, she sent me a note, and it was very much about, "This might seem kind of strange, but I'm supposed to give you this book." And it was addressed to 'Tall Mary' because we were such casual friends.

So then I sat down and read it and I'm just like, "Oh my gosh. How could I not know? How could I not know?"Which, in a way, frustrated me because it's like, I've been a Catholic for 56 years. How can the Blessed Virgin Mary be appearing and I don't know about it? How can it not be on the news every night? Oh my gosh! How can it be?"

Then I wanted to know more so I went online and found Queen of Peace Productions and read about that. And then I got Mirjana's book, and I read that. And it was all absolutely wonderful like "I do believe" but it was also... it wasn't "I don't want to go" it was, "I don't have to go." But then it was very much a "despite the fact I don't feel that I have to go, it appears that I'm going." Because I needed things to line up, and they lined up. And then, certainly, you want to get ready for a pilgrimage, so you pray more and that was wonderful and wanting to pray more was wonderful. And then being here is amazing.

*Our Lady says, it is a time of great grace. I feel it is a tremendous time of great grace.*

Mary said, "Open your heart, I'll do the rest." So pray the Rosary and even if you're not doing it very well, pray the Rosary and I will help you pray the Rosary better. Then at the beginning of the year, I thought, why don't I pray the Rosary every day? And they're not all great, don't get me wrong, especially if I put them off until the end of the day.

But that's not me. Where did I get this desire to pray the Rosary? All of it? It is a time of great grace.

*~Mary, Washington USA*

I heard about Medjugorje in 1983 while in college from a priest friend. It turns out he was the same priest who married us and baptized all three of our kids. But I never really had a burning desire to come here.

The Blessed Mother didn't really play a significant role to me until Erin [my wife] came to Medjugorje. She always wanted me to come and I was really resistant to go at the time. Primarily because I was working and I had other priorities and if I was going to make a trip to Europe it was going to be somewhere fun but I agreed to come for her 50th birthday. Part of the reason I resisted to come, I think, is if you do something like this, and I knew the profound effect it had on [my wife], that our lives probably would change. And you get pretty comfortable living the way you are living. It's true, it has changed our lives, but it's definitely been for the positive. I had heard about Fatima and Lourdes and we finally got a chance to go to those places and they are wonderful. But those apparitions happened many many years ago in the past but what we are experiencing in Medjugorje is happening right now.

Not just with the visionaries, which is super special, but this whole community; they are living their faith. As we found out when you come here more often you get to meet some of the locals, and find out that they have real world problems. They have the same issues that everybody else has that would be in a small town.

They are witnesses of what the true Christian community is like and are an example for what we can bring back to our own communities. This is what we are trying to do, bring back a piece of Medjugorje. You can change the world. There's no question about that.

~*Shawn, California USA*

In 2010, I came to Medjugorje. It was just a very profound experience. I didn't know what to expect. I came with an open mind, without any expectations and I was just blown away.

We had four Legionary Priests that were just incredible. I did a general confession which lasted 2 hours and 45 minutes and the priest just cried with me; he was so patient and loving. I was so scared before, then he turned to me and was like, "Why? Why would you be scared?" and my heart melted in that moment.

My whole life changed. I knew one life before coming here – I am going to start crying now – and it was the most beautiful transformation. This joy filled my heart that was not of Earth; it came from somewhere else and life made sense.

I never wanted to go back to the way I was. I never wanted that feeling of joy to leave my soul. It was just beautiful, it was like God and the Blessed Mother came into me, came into my soul and woke me from my slumber.

I remember going home on the airplane and I sat next to someone that was an atheist and we just started this dialogue and he asked me about Medjugorje and he said, "Well, did you see the Blessed Mother?" and I said, "Well, I didn't physically see Her with my eyes, but I felt Her in my heart." I truly did feel Her in my heart so strongly. As soon as I told him that, I could feel Her in my heart. That was the first time I felt like I was evangelizing something. One of the priests that was in our group had mentioned that first time, that it was like a lamp that burns oil and after it burns for a while it starts to diminish, oil kind of lessens and you just have to keep refilling that oil. And that's what coming back to Medjugorje does, it kind of helps refill your oil. And I kind of looked at it the same way because by the end of that year, I just longed for Medjugorje so much. I longed to come back and thankfully I was able to come back. And Shawn [my husband] supported me in that.

~ *Erin, California USA*

**Erin:** I got home and I just tried to live my life but everything was different. Even the way related to my children and to Shawn [my husband]. He can probably tell you how I was changed. The kids thought I was crazy, they thought "What happened to Mom?" I became a church lady. I did bible studies and prayed the Rosary; I couldn't get enough. That's all the reading I wanted to do, is to feed my soul and learn more.

**Shawn:** She really went from being very lukewarm and going through the motions to being really on fire. And I didn't realize it at the time, it was a little annoying for the rest of us, but that was probably carrying the faith of the family on to the next place that we needed to get to, and certainly that we needed to get to as a couple.

**Erin:** I started really praying the last couple times before he came. My prayer was for our marriage to be blessed with this experience and that Mary would touch his heart. And I didn't think it would happen. Because he didn't want to come but he did, he came because it was my 50th birthday, and he came begrudgingly, sort of. Anyway, he came reluctantly, I would say.

I let him just have his space and kind of just go off on his own. Just so he could have his own experience. It was like watching a butterfly; he was like a caterpillar that went through all the stages. And all these people in the group kind of noticed it too. It was really incredible. We got home the beginning of November and he said I don't know about you but I have to go back to Medjugorje and then he gave us a trip back and we came in April and then we've been coming twice a year ever since and it's been awesome.

**Shawn:** Coming that first time was emotional. I committed to praying the Rosary while I was here, when I came for her birthday, and I've prayed the Rosary every day for the last 2 and a half almost 3 years. It's just become a priority for me because I know that there are fruits coming from it that I can't necessarily see right now. And you know, probably like most people that are honest, my faith goes up and down – real dryness periods – but I think it's the commitment. And the Rosary is an easy way for me to have that commitment every day, to offer it up and to ask for the Blessed Mother's intercession to take weak prayers and make them better.

**Erin:** Medjugorje has truly blessed our life as a couple, blessed our marriage, and I know it will bless our children, and it's already had an impact on our families too. It's a beautiful, beautiful grace.

He and I share this now. We're completely a unit, completely together in this journey, and learning our faith and practicing our faith. It's different; it's not like it's just me anymore off crazy. And it's not like he was just going through the rote motions with Sunday mass and that's it. Now it's definitely a lifestyle. It's part of our life. It's who we are.

**Shawn:** I think we've gotten lucky enough to realize there's so much goodness, grace, and brilliance in the Catholic faith that we didn't realize. Medjugorje was like the first chapter. It was the beginning of the book. And then you just keep turning the pages, and the more you dig, the more you find how much depth is really there, and that's been a fun journey that we can do together. It's pretty profound.

## OUR LADY'S MESSAGE TO MIRJANA ON JUNE 2, 2019

"Dear children, only a pure and an open heart will make it such that you may truly come to know my Son and that all those who do not know His love may come to know it through you. Only love will make you comprehend that it is stronger than death because true love conquered death and made it so that death does not exist.

My children, forgiveness is the most exalted form of love. You, as apostles of my love, must pray that you be strong in spirit and that you could comprehend and forgive. You, apostles of my love, by understanding and forgiveness, are giving an example of love and mercy. To be able to comprehend and forgive is a gift for which it is necessary to pray, and to nurture it.

By forgiveness you are showing that you know how to love. Just look, my children, how the Heavenly Father loves you with a great love, with understanding, forgiveness and justice—how He gives me, the Mother of your hearts, to you. And here I am among you to bless you with a motherly blessing, to call you to prayer, to fasting—to tell you to believe, to hope, to forgive, to pray for your shepherds, and above all to love without limits.

My children, follow me. My way is the way of peace and love, the way of my Son. It is the way that leads to the triumph of my heart. Thank you."

~Our Lady Queen of Peace, June 2

I had my luggage with me and the first thing I did is go to confession. And the priest said, "Oh I see you bring your luggage with you" and I said, "Actually my physical luggage and my whole life luggage." He just smiled at me. And then I was telling him my sins and a little about my life but somehow he said to me, "Where did you say your husband is from?" I said, "He's from Greece." and he said "You are from Mexico?" And I said, "Yes, when we got married, he promised over the Bible that we would raise the kids Catholic. He is a man of his word and he let me raise our kids Catholic."

I've always hoped my husband would participate in the faith with the family. I think he would be happier. My husband attended a boarding school run by Orthodox priests in his youth, and read the whole Bible in Greek. When I told the priest that, he said "I bet he has it all in his heart." He asked me if I knew how to speak Greek. I can understand some things and I learned to cook very well Greek food for him. He said "Well, I am going to tell you a few prayers in Greek so you pray with him in Greek. You can go on the internet and find these short prayers. Greeks have very good prayers about the mercy of God and about Our Lady. Then you start learning a little bit more and you will surprise him. And then perhaps like this he will open his heart to God."

When he told me that, I almost cried because it was so simple, so simple! And I could not believe I never thought about it. After 36 years married, I have another clue what to do. And when I return home, I am going to pray first to God to give me the right prayers to land into his heart. And then I will leave it all to Him, all to Jesus.

From now and on I am never going to tell him "I love you," I am going to tell him "s'agapo" ('I love you' in Greek). And I am never going to say "Gusito, my love" I am going to tell him "agapi mou" ('my love' in Greek).

~*Thelma, Texas USA*

**Mauricio:** It's been a long time since we went out together. We felt that Our Lady was calling us and I wanted to give thanks. It's been 3 years since my diagnosis and I have had many opportunities that many haven't had. I want to give thanks because I could be dead. I could be suffering greatly, and in reality, I am not. Everything was part of a plan. I did my part and the most important part was guided by the hand of God. He was putting the path for me to follow and here we are advancing.

**Claudia:** To deal with the emotional part of this illness, to see my children hurting, to see my husband hurting, I think the role of the caregiver carries a lot of the weight because you have to be the support in every way and get through it all. It's so hard and at the same time you pretend that there's nothing wrong.

**Mauricio:** Before, it was a taboo to talk about death and now I see death as a step to eternal life. I know I will reunite with all my loved ones who are there. If I go now, my loved ones here… I will see them there in time.

**Claudia:** For me it was an amazing experience to be with Mirjana, the visionary, not only to see her but to hear her and get to ask her questions. When I asked her if she has seen Heaven, she said yes. She said that Our Lady communicates not only through the heart, but that Mirjana can hear her with her ears. That was fascinating— to be with a person who has seen the love of Our Holy Mother.

**Mauricio:** You breathe in a lot of peace. You can see people from all over the world, with the same purpose, searching for a closeness to God and to the Virgin Mary.

**Claudia:** You feel you are touching Heaven. You can't explain it. Only in experiencing it you can live it.

~*Claudia & Mauricio, Mexico*

I first came to Medjugorje in 2004. I had a life or death, heaven or hell experience. I'd had an addiction to drugs at the time and was being gradually dragged away from that by the Lord because of this experience I had – it was the catalyst for me. Basically, in that experience it was, "if I were going to die right now, where was I going to go?" That was the question that the Lord posed to me. But I pretty much knew the outcome of that one very quickly without having to say it. I was like, "Please Lord I don't want to go there, but I know I absolutely deserve to go there." But he just kind of placed in my mind, "Say the Act of Contrition." So I said the Act of Contrition and that was the start, but it took me a year to get off drugs.

There was a guy I used to work with in a job, because I was a functioning addict, I had a job but I still did the drugs. He used to talk about Medjugorje a lot and the peace that he had. So I would say it was maybe 3-4 weeks before I came to Medjugorje. I gave up the drugs and come out here. I was blessed that I didn't have to go to a drying-out clinic or anything like that. When I came here, I experienced the most amazing peace that I'd never experienced in 24 years of my life at that stage. If my mother was here today, she'd say that, "My son left Ireland and somebody else came back - someone who was actually smiling for the first time." So she could see the change, there was no doubt. I've just kept coming back ever since. This is my 11th time here.   ~*Ferghal*

## OUR LADY'S MESSAGE TO MIRJANA ON JULY 2, 2019

"Dear children, according to the will of the merciful Father, I have given you, and will still give you, evident signs of my motherly presence.

"My children, this is a motherly desire for the healing of souls. This is a desire that every child of mine may have true faith, to live to see wondrous experiences, drinking from the spring of the words of my Son—the words of life.

"My children, my Son, by His love and sacrifice, brought the light of faith into the world and showed you the way of faith. Because, my children, faith elevates pain and suffering. "True faith makes prayer more sensitive, and does acts of mercy—a conversation, a gift of alms. "Those of my children who have faith—true faith—are happy despite everything because they live the beginning of heavenly happiness on earth. Therefore, my children, apostles of my love, I am calling you to give an example of true faith, to bring light where there is darkness, to live my Son.

"My children, as a mother I am telling you: you cannot go on the way of faith and follow my Son without your shepherds. "Pray that they may have the strength and the love to lead you. May your prayers always be alongside them. Thank you."

~Our Lady Queen of Peace, July 2

**iMedj Note:** Bobbie Jean Murray and Crystal Murray, featured *Where There Is Darkness* by Stella Mar Films, are the sisters of convicted murderer Steven Murray, a young man who kidnapped a Catholic priest in 2016. With him, they shared a tragic childhood that left deep wounds in their hearts.

The Murray sisters are not Catholic, which makes their Medjugorje experience all the more amazing. Bobbie Jean and Crystal arrived in Medjugorje on June 24, 2019 with Stella Mar Pilgrimages, and they were present at the July 2nd apparition to Mirjana Soldo. It was almost as if Our Lady acknowledged them when, in her message, she asked us all to "bring light where there is darkness."

Witnessing the apparition and being so close to Mirjana had a profound effect on the sisters, and Our Lady's words helped make their experience all the more profound.

Special thanks to Marilyn from Iowa for helping sponsor the Murray sisters' visit to Medjugorje—without ever having met them! After seeing the film *Where There is Darkness*, she felt in her heart that they should feel the peace from Medjugorje.

**Bobbie Jean:** I can't explain it. It was so real. I believe I got more faith right now than I've had in a long time. At first, I was like okay we are going to go up this hill, I didn't know what to expect. I had doubts. I don't know.

You can just feel that presence. When she looked up, it's like she was talking to her. I am glad Crystal and I did it together. I just think it would be amazing if she goes home and gets to that doctor and they are looking at her and say "there's nothing there," that they don't find any problem with her heart.

**iMedj Note:** Crystal suffers from health problems related to the abuse she endured in her childhood, and the traumatic effects from it, as told in our film *Where There Is Darkness*.

**Crystal:** It was beautiful. It was amazing. You could just feel the presence and I just started crying... immediately.

**Bobbie Jean:** It just came. You can't help it.

**Crystal:** I've never experienced anything like that before. And like she said, I think I have more faith now than probably ever.

**Bobbie Jean:** I also told her last night, I said it would be so cool if we get up on that hill and see our momma. And that didn't happen but I felt like she was there. After this, I kind of feel like I could just stay. I was so anxious to go home and leave and now I just want to stay.

*Before Mirjana's Apparition on 7-2-19*

*Scene from the film Where There is Darkness*

I'm going to be a senior in college at Walsh University. Our president and his wife are leading a pilgrimage for us, along with one of our priests [Father Denk].

They've done this a couple years. He's retiring so this will be their last one. They have been here multiple times. They planned the trip. We went to Rome before this and now we're here and then we're going to Lourdes.

I love it. We got in Saturday and it was late and we were like, "I don't know what we're gonna do tonight." But then we ran into Thelma (See page 53.) and she's like, "Let's go to the Blue Cross."

There was a group praying before us in either Spanish or Italian. We listened to them and then we went and did a prayer with Thelma and we sang the 'Ave Ave.' Being there all together at nighttime, it kicked off the time here perfectly.

## *Celebrating Mass every day has been such a blessing.*

It's so peaceful and everyone here is so pleasant. I'm half Croatian too so for me it's very special because it feels like home. I walked in the "pansion" here and it just felt like my grandparent's house. You can feel the Spirit present, and everyone is just so loving.

I'm a biology major, and I'm going to be starting physical therapy school. So I have 3 more years. Most of my classmates, we've been friends or at least know each other, but I've gotten to know people better and in different ways. And we have fun. I wish everybody could experience Medjugorje. It's a different, unique, humble, beautiful place.

~*Daniella, USA*

I just graduated college. I double majored in theology and interdisciplinary studies and minored in communications history and Spanish – which is a lot. Starting in June, I'm going to be a youth minister at St. Francis of Assisi, which is a parish outside of Cleveland.

My family isn't Croatian, but my adopted family is. I've grown up around it, knowing about Our Lady of Medjugorje, and I've always wanted to come so as soon as they said, "We're going to Medjugorje." I knew I had to come on the trip.

Growing up, we had the faith in the house. My mom works at a parish. My dad is a deacon. I'm going to be a youth minister. So the faith was super present in the house, but we never prayed the Rosary as a family or had a strong devotion to Mary as a family. I was reading Mirjana's book, and she talks about her 2nd of the month apparitions. My mom's birthday is December 2nd and my best friend's birthday is May 2nd and my birthday is March 2nd. So there's things that Mary has come and said on my birthday. And toward the end of the book, it says, "On March 2nd 1997, I was here. And it was one of the first apparitions I did at the Blue Cross. And this is what Mary said."

My birth date – like actual birth date – is March 2nd, 1997. It was just this thing that Mary was saying to me too. The other night when I went there, I was just overcome with emotion to know that we have a relentless Father that pursues us, but there's also this relentless Mother that pursues us all the way as well.
~Cari, USA

*Our Lady's message to Mirjana on March 2, 1997: "Dear children, pray for your brothers who haven't experienced the love of the Father, for those whose only importance is life on earth. Open your hearts towards them and see in them my Son, who loves them. Be my light and illuminate all souls where darkness reigns. Thank you for having responded to my call."*

This is my first time here. It's beautiful and the people have been so welcoming. The first experience that we had was walking with Miki [a local guide]. Miki's just awesome because he shares from his heart and he was here when the apparitions began. Walking up the hill together with him and praying the Rosary was a beautiful experience for me, and I know also for the teens. We have Catholics and even a few non-Catholics. It was beautiful for all of them. There are 19 students; 24 of us total.

I have a ministry and the whole focus is teaching people how to pray. It's called the Prodigal Father and it's all about experiencing God the Father's love. So hearing [visionary] Mirjana talk and what she said about how important it is just to feel God's love and to pray for those that aren't experiencing that, was beautiful for me because that's my whole desire.

*I feel, as a priest, I've gotten to experience His love in a very special way, and I just want to share that.*

For me, it was a real confirmation of focusing even more on helping people experience God's love for real. I try to make it all free. That's part of the 'prodigal,' that God gives freely. We usually think of the son as the prodigal one, but God is even more prodigal. He gives us His grace, even if we waste it. He just keeps giving and giving with Mass and the sacraments and confession and prayer.

I studied film and media in undergrad at Cleveland State University. I wanted to be a director. I had the call for a long time, since I was a child, but I finally was able to say yes and I left all that behind. But now I'm kind of getting back into it. Walsh University has a studio, and part of my teaching people how to pray is using media, using smartphones. I have an app that I've created. To have this device in our hands, that people can access scripture, they can access all these teachings, guided meditations, prayer. We're already so hooked to it that we gotta be using it. So that's my mission.

~ *Father Michael Denk, USA*

I was really moved by the message and Our Blessed Mother. I was looking for healing in my heart. I was looking for answers on how I could best support my daughter who at the time was struggling in college lifestyle.

I came on pilgrimage to Medjugorje and I learned about the 5 stones. That was one thing I took back with me. I thought to myself, "I got nothing to lose."

I went home and really started to live them. I started fasting on Fridays. I started going to daily Mass, which was a big deal for me. I read Scripture daily, on my phone, and prayed the Rosary. I had nothing to lose and started implementing all of it, and it just changes your life.

My husband came back with me the following year. We came home from that trip and my husband and I started fasting for our kids and what they were dealing with.

I've been fasting now for 15 years. It's allowed me to view things so differently. I thought I was fasting for my family, but really in so many ways I was fasting for myself. I was visiting with my priest and he said, "I bet you are able to do some of those things because of your fasting.

*I think fasting is the hardest prayer and one that I feel has been very impactful to my prayer life.*

Christ Our Life is a fruit of Medjugorje. It came about by the fact that we were so passionate about Medjugorje and praying the Rosary.

As I was praying the Rosary, it came to my heart that we need a conference in the heartland of America that would help us to understand what we believe as Catholic Christians.

I called my best friend Marilyn, because I knew I couldn't do it on my own. Marilyn and I have been bringing pilgrims to Medjugorje for the past 15 years. She felt she was having the same calling and so together we got ahold of our Monsignor Joe and we created Christ Our Life.
In 2008, we were in Medjugorje and we ran into Magnus from Mary's Meals and we invited him to the Christ Our Life conference and every conference since. We had no idea the ripple effects the conference would make in people's lives and how it would help to support the work of Mary's Meals.

We thought it would be a one-time conference, and that we'd invite Mirjana Soldo as well as other speakers who would move hearts and change lives. We thought instead of bringing 7,000 people to the other side of the world, maybe we could create and bring a Medjugorje Christ Our Life moment to Iowa and the people there.

We invited Mirjana and she couldn't make it, so we tried again in 2012, and 2014, and 2016, and 2018. I think we were wearing her down. It was one of the moments, when we thought, "Do we ask her again? This is getting humiliating." Then we asked her again and she said yes! We are so excited that she's given her yes in 2020 and we are going to fill the arena.

~*Ellen Iowa, USA*

*Marilyn and Ellen from Iowa, directors of Christ Our Life conference with Mirjana Soldo.*

## OUR LADY'S MESSAGE TO MIRJANA ON AUGUST 2, 2019

"Dear children, great is the love of my Son. If you were to come to know the greatness of His love, you would never cease to adore and thank Him. He is always alive with you in the Eucharist, because the Eucharist is His Heart. The Eucharist is the heart of faith.

He has never left you. Even when you tried to go away from Him, He has not [left] you. That is why my motherly heart is happy when I watch how you—filled with love—return to Him, when I see that you are coming to Him by the way of reconciliation, love, and hope.

My motherly heart knows that when you set out on the way of faith, you are shoots—buds. But along with prayer and fasting you will be fruits, my flowers, apostles of my love; you will be carriers of light and will illuminate all those around you with love and wisdom. My children, as a mother I am imploring you: pray, think, and contemplate. Everything beautiful, painful, and joyful that happens to you—all of this makes you grow spiritually, so that my Son may grow in you.

My children, surrender yourselves to Him, believe Him, trust in His love, let Him lead you. Let the Eucharist be the place where you will feed your souls, and afterwards, will spread love and truth—will bear witness to my Son. Thank you."

~Our Lady Queen of Peace, August. 2

These two people from our parish, Mr. Todd and Miss Angie, their daughter Meghan had cancer and she came here. [Visionary] Mirjana had asked her to come to the apparition. And she felt she was invited to bring youth back here after. But she had passed away. So, they started Meghan's Mission to bring a group of youth to the Youth Fest. We have 7.

iMedj note: To Jude's surprise, Mirjana invited him to be near her during the apparition in the area typically reserved for priests and the sick.

We walked up the hill through the barricades and that's when it hit me. I was like, "Dang, there's like thousands of people out here, and I'm gonna be within five feet of her." I was completely mind-blown.

I got up there and they asked me, "Do you want to sit or do you want to kneel?" And I said, "I kind of want to kneel." And she's like, "Okay, if you kneel, you're kneeling for the whole time." So, I pulled out my phone, I looked at the time, and I was like, "I think I got that." It was like 6:35. So I kneeled the whole entire time [9:00 AM].

This is the crazy part. They were saying the Rosary in different languages. I prayed, I said, "Mary, don't make me look like a fool. I don't know their language. So if you could help me out." And then literally right when I prayed that ... the woman sitting next to me, she grabbed the microphone and said the Rosary in English. She prayed the whole decade in English and I was completely mind-blown. And I was like, "Alright, so she's definitely here." The feeling was definitely there. It was just amazing to experience it. It's definitely different, but it's good different.    ~Jude, Louisiana USA

I was here June of 2017 with a group. It was my mom, my older brother, and I, and she surprised us. She was like, "Hey, we're going to Medjugorje with Father Anthony in June. It'll be great." Immediately, I was like, "You're out your tree Mom. I'm not going. What is there in this Bosnia? I don't even know how to pronounce it." So I, up until we got here, was 'grumples.' I didn't want to be here. I was 15 at the time.

The first thing we do is come across the street to [visionary] Mirjana and we hear her testimony. Before she came out to speak to us, we're praying the Rosary. My heart started to race and my head was pounding and it was like I couldn't keep my eyes open. It just got so heavy. I was sitting in my mom's lap so she felt me tense up and was like, "What's up?" And I couldn't speak. I couldn't answer.

As they kept praying the Rosary, the entire dining hall was filled with people from all around the world. And it's just tears coming down my face. At that point, Mirjana had come out and started giving her testimony. The whole time she's speaking, I'm just crying and crying. And it's really in one ear, out the other. I don't know what's going on. I'm there, but I'm not there. I couldn't even feel my mom under me, sitting in her lap anymore. We went about our day, and then we were going on a walking tour of the church grounds. We're on the side of St. James by all the confessionals and I went up to my priest and he's like, "What's wrong?" And I just broke down. And I was like, "I don't know what happened to me." I explained it to him as best as I could, and he stopped me, looked at me dead in my eyes, and he said, "You felt Heaven." This new life was just thrust upon me. From that point on, Mary was like, "I'm not letting go of you. I'm gonna make you my warrior — my prayer warrior."

I visited the Shrine of Our Lady of Guadalupe, and there I was given my vocation. It was a vision of me holding a child and leading children of all different ages and sizes and ethnicities from all over the world to Our Lady here in Medjugorje.  ~*Dena, Louisiana USA*

It changed my daughter Meghan's life. She realized how precious life was to her. She always wanted to live, but then she wanted to live for Jesus.

Meghan was so angry. And then about ten months before she came here, she started realizing there was more to life. She started really coming back to church and really starting to read scripture a little bit. But then when she came and knelt with Mirjana is when she got her full conversion to where she realized, "This has changed my life. I'm going to Heaven. I'm doing everything that I need to do to get my spot in Heaven."

She always made these comments after that apparition. She would always say, "I know." She knew what was happening. I don't know what happened because she never told me, but it was like she knew what her mission was.

*Angie's daughter Meghan--diagnosed with a terminal illness--came to Medjugorje Oct. 2018*

She prayed for nonbelievers, she prayed for the poor souls in Purgatory. I mean, she really dedicated herself to praying for everybody she knew. It was just a huge conversion for her.

She would call me and ask me, "Mom, are you ready to pray the Rosary?" Because she was getting so sick. "Mom, will you come and read the Bible to me? What book are we gonna read from tonight?" And a lot of times, she'd fall asleep. I'd be reading to her and I would say, "Are you with me?" And she'd say, "I'm with you."

And then I'd read another couple chapters, you know the Bible's kinda long, then she'd say, "I'm with you, Mom. Keep going." After a little while, she'd be knocked out. Then she'd wake up, "Okay!" I'd start reading to her again.

I really think she's still praying for our family and praying for nonbelievers and praying for the poor souls in Purgatory. When she went up to Apparition Hill, she had three papers, and she stayed up for hours in Mirjana's hotel just reading over that. She didn't want to forget to pray for anybody. I still have it. She just has notes — Pray for this one; pray for that one. Pray for my parents and their marriage. Pray for my goddaughter that she stays pure and that she knows God. Because she can be angry. Meghan was like a second mother to her, so she just didn't understand.

When we were all here in Medjugorje, Meghan came to me and was telling me about Youth Fest, and she said, "We need to bring kids from our parish." So as she got sicker and sicker, it was something she really talked about, my granddaughter coming with us. I mean, she didn't know if she would live or die, but she always talked like she would live. She fought to the very end. But in the end, she knew exactly where she was going.

When she passed away, we just picked up from where she spoke about doing it, and we made it into a reality. It was Jacques that came up with the name of 'Meghan's Mission.' We have been so hyped up about Medjugorje in our parish. I would say 90% of the people in our area know what it is now because of us sharing it all on Facebook and talking to them at church. We went to other churches to ask for donations.

We were going around to local businesses soliciting money to bring our kids, and in two months' time we got every penny and some. Because Meghan ended up being so sick, we had her wedding in December, she passed away in January, so we didn't really start fundraising until February. We had to have all the funds in by the end of March so we did yard sales, we asked people on the altar at the end of mass, we made little spiels to get people to donate to them, we knocked on local businesses' doors, we did all of that.

As a parent, I always tell anybody because they ask me, "How do you do it? How do you keep a smile on your face? Why are you so happy?" And I just say, "Well, she's in Heaven." I know she is. She's where she belongs.

~*Angie, Louisiana USA*

I ended up coming on the trip because my nanny and my best friend was Meghan. Since she passed away, I kind of wanted to come for her so she could come through me because she wanted to come back so bad, and she unfortunately passed away before she got the chance to do that. This place inspired her a lot.

She was my aunt. We had a really, really, really close bond. She was my best friend in the whole world.

I wanted to experience Medjugorje for her. I didn't expect it to be so beautiful. It's a very pure and uncorrupted place. Also, I didn't expect to be so spiritually impacted. I was a very big skeptic. I barely really believed in God.

At the apparition I didn't expect anything to happen to me. I just expected it to be almost like a placebo effect, like people only think the Blessed Mother is here because people say that she is, you know? And then when she ended up coming down, I did have a lot of physical reaction but also spiritual reaction. And from then on I also got the signs form my nanny and it was just a beautiful thing.

I ended up speaking to Mirjana about the experience. I will never forget what she said. I was like, "Your book [*My Heart Will Triumph*] brought my nanny here and it brought a lot of peace. Your apparitions and your kindness influence a lot of people. What you have done and what you continue to do gave my nanny a lot of peace when she passed away."

She had a spiritual connection with God, and she would always say, "I get it now," because of what Mirjana does. And then I told her that what she does, through her kindness, brings people here, and it brought me here, and now I'm a believer. And just two days ago, I wasn't.

She ended up crying because she was like, "Now you make me cry." Mirjana was saying it's so important for me to believe because of how young I am, and eventually this is going to be my world. The young people need to believe and impact people because every day people's faith is dwindling. I didn't know that all of the visionaries have a different mission, and that Mirjana's mission was for the nonbelievers. Because that's what my nanny prayed for the most was the nonbelievers. So, I thought it was a weird thing that they both had the same motivation, spiritually.
~*Alayna, Louisiana USA*

Meghan's Mission Youth Group from Louisiana joined
Stella Mar Pilgrimages to Medjugorje in August 2019

There's a lot of things that came together where it was like, "Wow, Mary is really calling me to go." I didn't know that Medjugorje existed. Dena first mentioned it in theatre class, and I started to think about it, but I'm just thinking to myself, "There's no way I'm leaving the country." I've never left the country before. So this is a first. And then I knew that my mother couldn't come and that was gonna freak her out. So I was like, "There's absolutely no way that I'm going." But it still stayed on my mind and I wasn't sure why. And then later in catechism class, we received a paper that was talking about Medjugorje, and they said that the next class, we're all gonna go to the auditorium and there's gonna be a talk about Medjugorje. I was like, "Okay, yeah, that's kind of weird."

We went there and Dena was giving a testimony, and she just poured her heart out. I was freaking out because there were a lot of things that came together for me to know that I had to go. As soon as the talk was done, I was like, "Mom, I have to go." And she let me go. It's been amazing. I've grown closer to the Blessed Mother than I've ever been before. I struggle to pray the Rosary. I pray every now and then, not as often as I can, just whenever I have a problem or in bed to go to sleep.

I had a one-decade rosary and it was made with a chain. It was the one that I was praying with the whole trip and I prayed a lot of Rosaries on it and the chain turned to gold. And I know that's a thing that happens here a lot. It never happened to me so I was kind of freaking out.

And then the other day, during Mirjana's talk, I felt Mary call me to do something with the rosary. She wanted me to give it to Mateo. I think he's sick. He has a deformity in his face. So, I gave it to him, but I didn't want to because I felt like it was special to me and I didn't want to get rid of it. But she kept tugging at my heart and I feel like I would feel worse if I didn't give it to him. So, I did what She said. I told him the Blessed Mother wants him to have this. I told him that the chain had started to turn to gold.

~*Mathew, Louisiana USA*

**Hayden:** I was really excited to camp out.

**Amy:** I was not excited about camping out, but they said, "Is there anybody who wants to camp out on the hill?" and I looked at Hayden, I looked at my friend Sylvia, and they were just like, "Yes." So I was like, "Okay, yes. I'll do it." So we decided to do it.

**Hayden:** It was so uncomfortable. We bought those little mats that roll out, and we had holes in them because of the sticks. Actually, can I tell the worm story?

**Amy:** I knew that she was gonna say the worm story. I knew it.

**Hayden:** So, I'm under the tree laying down, and I hear something hit the mat next to me. I felt it and I was like, "What was that?" I pick it up, and it's a worm so I'm like, "I'm gonna put it on Amy." So, I put the worm on her.

**Amy:** And then I took it, and I threw it on somebody else. I didn't know what it was. I picked it up, and I was like, "I don't even know." And I just threw it. She goes, "That was a worm." I was like, "Oh great." Anyway, disgusting.

**Hayden:** I thought, "I prayed for a sign, and God threw a worm at me."

**Amy:** You realize that everybody that is there and who starts filing in, that they're all coming and waiting for their Mother to arrive. So it was just exciting. They were doing all this singing. I was so moved by this beautiful girl. She was blind, and her voice just penetrated my spirit. And that song stayed in my head for the rest of the week. But leading up to it, just the excitement of it. Then when Mary appeared, and it fell silent, you realized why you were on the mountain for thirteen hours. Because here She is, and this peace and this love just is undeniable.

**Hayden:** Leading up to it, I was like, "I'm ready. I'm ready." And then when it fell silent, my heart started beating really fast. It was when I saw Mirjana look up. It was just incredible. I couldn't even think clearly. I actually had to look away because it was so overwhelming. I'm so glad we did that. I'm glad we camped out.

I always understand every invitation as God's call. So, I went home and began to preach about Medjugorje for the first time after I came here last October. That was about my fourth or fifth visit, and that was the first time I understood the importance of Medjugorje. After I read visionary Mirjana's book [*My Heart Will Triumph*], she put everything into perspective. It was as if little Blessed Mother was talking to me personally. It woke me up from sleep. I have tried to tell every priest and every bishop that I meet, just be open to it. Something's happening right now in our time and you're not paying attention. I would invite everyone to come to Medjugorje when we still have time.

And some parishioners were wondering, why do I need to bring the children all the way across the world. I said, "They need to see it so they understand how important this is." Because all they know is the civilization they're born in — in America. It was necessary for them to see 50,000 other kids praising in the heat, no air conditioning, no comfort, sitting on the grass, and still going to church. If we had no air conditioning in church in America, I'm sure nobody would come on Sunday. But they were willing to suffer all that and just watch other people believe too. And they're going back to America very different kids.

I couldn't preach it. I couldn't just tell them. They had to see it and feel it and know it.

And now I can tell you that we have a firm foundation for the future of the Church in my parish. These kids will never forget why they should pray the Rosary, why they should go to church and be very convinced Christians.

The Youth Festival is about seeking God. It's also about young minds seeking for truth. Jesus says, "I am the Way and the Truth and the Life. No one comes to the Father except through me." Seeking truth is seeking Christ. So, I would propose that to every young person today, come to every Youth Festival, every year.

~*Fr. Anthony, Louisiana USA*

**Kelly:** I said, "I don't think it's my time. I'll go to Medjugorje when I'm older." Jacques and I always wanted to go to Paris because I'm an artist and I have an architecture history minor. But after talking to Meghan about it, I was like, "Jacques, we have to go to Medjugorje." Meghan and I went to high school together so just knowing her and seeing her spiritual transformation. She was so moved by Medjugorje. And Jacques was like, "No. We're going to Paris…" I asked him twice, and then finally he came to me and said, "We have to go."

**Jacques:** Yeah, I don't know what the calling was, but something just said we gotta go. So that's what we did.

**Kelly:** He said he wanted come back before I did. The first two days, he said, "I wanna come back again." Because people always say, once you come, you want to come back.

When we decided we were gonna come, because our anniversary was a week ago, I said we should go up to Cross Mountain and have our marriage blessed by Father Anthony. Then, the other day, Father said, "Do you want to do Apparition Hill?" And we had watched someone propose up there the first day we walked up there. It was just really sweet and I had a change of heart. So, I was like, "We need to do that"… It was really sweet, and [Father Anthony] gave us a blessing and did the marriage vows with us. We were holding a cross because I heard that it's a custom for people who get married in Medjugorje to buy a cross and then hold the cross while you say your vows and then hang it in the home. I wanted to do that because it's unique to the place and it will be a memento for us.

**Jacques:** I've spent the last few days trying to put my experience of Medjugorje into words and I've been unsuccessful. For a person that truly loves to talk, it's been quite humbling. I can say that there is definitely a level of peace in Medjugorje like no other place I've ever been. A peace that can't be described, only experienced.

**Cheryl:** Everybody thought I was nuts. "What? Where are you going?" I was trying to go to Fatima. I wanted somebody to go with me and nobody could go. While I was googling stuff, I came across something about Medjugorje. Then I decided I didn't need anybody to go with me. "I can do this by myself." Coming during Youthfest last year. I mean, to see the flags waving and all these people. To see the confession lines. I just wish I could get my own kids to come.

The heat scared me, but I'm here. It scared me last year and it scared me this year, but actually I wasn't bothered by the heat as much as I thought. We did all our hiking in the middle of the night. I was scared out of my brains by myself until the next morning when I woke up and I met my fellow pilgrims. They're like my sisters and brothers now. I love them. We just had a reunion last weekend. And they're very jealous that I'm going back.

**Ellen:** I felt an internal call after I read *My Heart Will Triumph*. I've known about Medjugorje since the early 90s. I've followed the messages. When I met Cheryl, my new friend since April 13th...and then we started chatting, there were things in common, then she said, "Would you like to go on a pilgrimage to Poland with me?"

I said, "Oh, you don't want me to go on a pilgrimage to Poland with you." Because my knees are in a lot of pain; it's difficult for me to walk. I hate to fly, and I don't have a passport.

We were at Divine Mercy Sunday, they alerted us that the pilgrimage to Poland might not run because of a lack of subscription. So, we talked about what we might do, and I said, "Would you like to go back to Medjugorje?" And she said, "Oh yeah, I would go in a heartbeat."

Being brought up Catholic, Mum always had us pray the Rosary in the evenings and also developing my own personal devotion to Our Lady. I haven't seen Mum for more than a year now. She arrived Friday from South Africa and right away we were on the plane together.

I belong to the religious order of the Missionary Oblates of Mary Immaculate and I am from South Africa. I've been a priest for 7 and a half years and I am currently in Rome completing a licentiate in sacred scripture.

Our course in sacred scripture focuses on the original languages, the language itself, and the message the Bible is trying to convey through the original language. ... the very words the angel spoke to Mary when he announced the words "full of grace" in that context doesn't mean that she is full of grace at that moment but that she had been full of grace at the moment of her conception – from her very existence. When she was conceived in St. Anne's womb, at that very moment Mary was full of grace.

Mary herself speaks and gives her own prophecy "from this day forward all generations will call me blessed" and that prophecy is being lived out at this moment and in a very special way here in Medjugorje.

To experience the peace of the place and meet people from all over the world – that's the beauty of our Catholic faith, the source of our faith brings us together, the Eucharist and the Rosary and so that's what has been really inspiring to me. I am definitely coming back.

~ *Fr. Sebastian, South Africa*

## OUR LADY'S MESSAGE TO MIRJANA ON SEPTEMBER 2, 2019

"Dear children, pray! Pray the Rosary every day— that wreath of flowers which, as a mother, directly connects me with your pains, sufferings, desires, and hopes.

Apostles of my love, I am with you through the grace and the love of my Son, and I am asking for prayers of you. The world is in such need of your prayers for souls to be converted. With complete trust, open your hearts to my Son, and in them He will inscribe the summary of His words— which is love. Live in an unbreakable connection with the Most Sacred Heart of my Son.

My children, as a mother, I am telling you that it is high time for you to kneel before my Son to acknowledge Him as your God, the center of your life. Offer gifts to Him— that which He most loves— which is love towards neighbor, mercy, and pure hearts.

Apostles of my love, many of my children still do not acknowledge my Son as their God; they have not yet come to know His love. But you, with your prayer pronounced from a pure and open heart, by the gifts which you offer to my Son, will make even the hardest hearts open.

Apostles of my love, the strength of prayer pronounced from the heart—a powerful prayer full of love— changes the world. Therefore, my children: pray, pray, pray. I am with you. Thank you."

~Our Lady Queen of Peace, September. 2

Back in the 50s, *I watched The Song of Bernadette*. I was so taken with that when I was about 8 years old, watching the movie, I said, "If Our Lady ever comes again, tell me." And She did.

*I right away knew this place was real — from the heart.*

So, I came in 1988 when it was still communist here, and I said, "I don't know what I'm doing here, but I know." I never had doubt that Our Lady was here. My favorite saint is Saint Bernadette. I owe everything to her, from that time, and she kept her promise. It's been a tough life. I was a scout in Vietnam.

I had the greatest dog on earth in Vietnam. It was this dog with a saint behind it. It was the meanest freaking dog on earth, yet totally obedient and loving toward me. Nothing else could get near me. And it chased things in Vietnam that broke up everything and saved everybody. Because I'd have to fly out and get guys out of trouble.

I was a scout, just like in the Old West, but in the Old West you could see a long way. In a jungle you can't see a long way. You can only see a short way. And that dog would go, and there'd be an ambush set up, and it'd scare the hell out of them and they would all scatter. They were ready to kill everybody, and we'd come upon the ambush and they'd leave. They'd drop their weapons; they'd drop stuff because that dog I had was terrible and terrifying.

I never lost anybody that I led — in or out of battle. All were unharmed, my whole year in Vietnam. Thirty-eight missions, and not one person was wounded. And we saw conflict, but the enemy scattered. That dog was scaring everybody except me. And I remembered, it all came back to me in what we've got to be in life for our shepherds and for the sheep. We have to be that kind of dog.

We have to be ready to protect our shepherds and to go out for the sheep.

And that's what Our Lady's told me in Medjugorje. Always be ready now. Because we now have entered into this moment, and the moment is the most extraordinary moment in the history of all time. It's now. If we follow Our Lady and we do what She says, She will definitely lead us and strengthen us for whatever our call is.

That call, it goes way back when I was a kid. And it was very innocent. I just wanted to see Our Lady, and so in 1988 when I went to Cross Mountain, I was by myself in the middle of the night. I went up there, and I got to the top maybe one o'clock in the morning. Back then it was trails; it was just dirt. And I went up there and I sat and I had that one experience that lives with me my whole life. It wasn't visual, but there are very many powerful things that God can do if your heart's open. And so I sat there until I saw the break of dawn. And I was the only one on the mountain all night. In 1988, August 15th. Back when there weren't many people here.

Guard your shepherds right now. They really need it. I feel for them greatly. They need the protection of the dogs and they need the respect of the sheep. We need to be very careful because the wolves are gathering and we're going to have to be ready for them. They're coming and they're going to do everything they can. So you've gotta be ready wherever you're at. Just like a military. Just like a scout.

*And the only way to get there is the Rosary.*

~*Neil, USA*

**Christian:** Our mom just asks us, "Do you guys want to go on a pilgrimage to Medjugorje?" We were like, "Eh, maybe. Maybe not." Like two days later, she said, "Yeah, alright. You're going. It's booked. The flight is booked. Everything is booked."

**Jeanna:** I think we just didn't know what to expect. We knew it would be okay, but then being here, the life of Christ is sincerely alive. You can sense the presence of Christ here. It's like a little dome of Heaven on Earth.

**Christian:** You can definitely feel it. It's definitely not just another random European city. It's definitely special.

**Jeanna:** We've seen so many miracles already this week. We saw the miracle of the sun. [Visionary Mirjana] has the face and the eyes of someone who has seen a piece of Heaven.

**Christian:** And she's just super sweet and so kind and caring. She has a big heart and you can just tell she's such a great person to be around. It was 100% worth [our parents'] time and effort and money to put the whole thing together and send us off. It definitely wasn't a waste. I had a little bit of skepticism just because all my friends are...They all think it's bogus. But being here just squashed all of that.

I was in Medjugorje when Pure in Heart gave a talk at the youth festival. It really resonated with me because it aligned with a commitment I'd made in my teenage years, but I hadn't thought about it much after that. I could see the real reason why Theology of the Body is so important, especially in today's society.

I felt very blessed to hear that message when I did, whereas a lot of people in Catholic and secular schools didn't hear about it (chastity) at all. I took it as a gift to be told about God's plan for our love lives.

I felt as though I'd been entrusted with this gift and it's something special to be able to share it with people and pass it on to them so they can know about it, share it, and themselves live that life.

When I first started giving these talks, I thought people might not know how to take it, they might not receive the presentation. The response was really good. I wasn't expecting that. Even if you give a talk and touch only a few, the entire talk is worth it, even if it is just one or two hearts.

When I was in Medjugorje, I was given an invitation to attend the canonization of John Paul II in Rome. When I went over, I remembered everything from his teaching in Theology of the Body. He is an amazing saint who really does a lot for the youth with World Youth Day and Theology of the Body. I reflected on that afterwards and that strengthened my resilience and my faith in belief in his teaching. So, I attribute it a bit to the intercession of John Paul II as well. Being in Medjugorje and receiving the invite to attend the canonization all kind of fit together, being that I first learned about Pure in Heart here in Medjugorje.

*~Warwick, Australia*

I believe in logic and science but you can take logic and science and shove it over a cliff — clouds don't form any faces. In 2016, I was filming the sun and 20 minutes to 7, when the Virgin Mary makes an apparition everyone kneels down but on this particular occasion, a cloud covers the sun...changes into a three dimensional face, nose, eyes, mouth and a cigarette in its mouth and I was the one smoking a cigarette. Guilty as charged.

From there I had to radically change my whole life because clouds don't form many faces.

I think the Virgin Mary's given me enough signs to make that transition from a life of secularism and a life that is more conducive to holiness.

But it is a hard transition to make, I am still struggling with it. You know my body sometimes still rejects it. I am not what you call, one of these happy clappy's, you know. I am a dour Scotsman and I am proud of it! ... I have always had a great devotion and love for the Virgin Mary, a great respect for Her. From that time onwards, that cloud in the sky, I've really made a considerate effort to try change.

Just recently my twin sister died. All of my family are all dead now. I've got no one. I feel a lot of loneliness. My way of thinking is if I obtain this certain high degree of holiness then I could never be lonely, if I got Christ and Mary in my life. I know what the truth is now. I knew I had to radically change my life. I am the black sheep of the family. I had to stop the womanizing, stop the drinking, radically change.

The woman that I was donating my blood, she was like "Oh you have the rarest blood in the world." Then I googled that, and guess who else is AB? Jesus. On the Turin shroud. He's AB positive. I am rarer, I'm AB negative. I am not trying to compare myself to Jesus. I can't turn water into wine, I can't walk on water, trust me I am not comparing myself to Jesus. I just find it odd.

~Paul, Scotland

**Jeannie:** I saw the film Apparition Hill a few years ago and I absolutely fell in love with the story. Funny enough Nicole sent me an email saying that she was going to Medjugorje and asked if I wanted to go. I told my husband how badly I wanted to go and he really encouraged me to. So here we are! It's been such a blessing, well actually, today was a triple blessing because we prayed the Rosary on Apparition Hill with Ivan (with a thousand other people, haha), we heard Jackov give his talk this morning, and then we had Father Leon, who is hysterical, give his talk to the pilgrims. We both read *My Heart Will Triumph* by Mirjana before coming. Everybody should read it! I want to buy bulk issues and give them out to people. All of the visionaries exuded so much joy and love. I just think that if we met Mary face-to-face every day, how holy would we be?

**Nicole:** I read some books from Wayne Weible years ago and that's how I got introduced to the apparitions. It was one of those "pie in the sky" maybe someday I'll get their sort of things that eventually just worked out perfectly. God works out all the details, the place where I work is shut down for a week and a half, which is the same time that I am here, so I didn't have to take any additional time off. It was meant to be, and I am just so thankful. I began praying and asking that a friend would come along with me. I ask Our Lady if she would remove any obstacles for the friend that would be coming. Then finally Jean, after just mentioning it, called me weeks later and said she was coming!

**Jeannie:** I'm so glad we came together, this way our brains will fill in for each other and help us remember things we heard and saw.

**Nicole:** Being able to share this experience will be huge. Unless you've been here it's hard to explain, and having someone to talk about it with is such a consolation.

## OUR LADY'S MESSAGE TO MIRJANA ON OCTOBER 2, 2019

"Dear children, The will and the love of the Heavenly Father make it so that I am among you, that I, with a motherly love, may help the growth of faith in your heart, for you to be able to truly comprehend the purpose of earthly life and the greatness of the heavenly one.

My children, the earthly life is the way to eternity, to truth, and to life— to my Son. I desire to lead you on that way. You, my children— you who always thirst for more love, truth, and faith— need to know that there is only one spring from which you can drink. It is trust in the Heavenly Father; it is trust in His love.

Abandon yourselves completely to His will and do not be afraid. Everything that is best for you, everything that leads you to eternal life, will be given to you. You will comprehend that the purpose of life is not always to want and take, but to love and give. You will have true peace and true love. You will be apostles of love. By your example, you will make it so that my children who do not know my Son and His love may desire to come to know Him.

My children, apostles of my love, adore my Son with me and love Him above all. Always strive to live in His truth. Thank you."

~Our Lady Queen of Peace, October 2

I first came to Medjugorje when I was 15 or 16, now I've just turned 20. I grew-up Catholic, my family was really strict in their faith, but I was hanging around guys who weren't really into their faith at all, I kind of struggled. I was at a Catholic school and at that stage we had the Franciscan Friars of the Renewal (CFR's). The year before I'd first gone to Medjugorje, the friars served as Irish-school chaplains, and during this time I connected with the RE (Religious Education) department of our school and they gave me a little background on Medjugorje and they invited me along. I thought I might as well give it a try, I'd been into my faith, but I never thought I'd go any further than what it was.

So, I went to Medjugorje with the school and it was an absolutely beautiful experience. Whenever I'm back home, you don't see what you see in Medjugorje. Every person you walked past here, there's a smile on their face. When we came, we were with the Friars of the Renewal, and before we came out, I thought there was going to be a lot of prayer, a lot of worship, etc. But when I came it was completely different. There was a lot of games and singing, a lot of good joking and banter.

The real key to my conversion in Medjugorje was confessions. I went to confession with Father Colombo, CFR, and I had my first ever proper confession. I always went down the list and said I cursed here and there, using bad words. But when I went to Father Colombo for the first time, I really opened my heart to what could come, to what I could get from the Lord. It changed me completely, I was able to be more vulnerable with the Lord and trust him completely. When I came home from Medjugorje I would go to the prayer room at my school with the Blessed Sacrament. I would go there and just pray for more and more, asking the Lord just to bless me and give me more strength.

I began teaching myself guitar, then I met up with Father Colombo who is himself a fantastic worship leader. He taught me everything I know, and I've come such a long way to be where I am today. I've done mission work and played worship music in Lebanon, Belgium, and Medjugorje. I am so blessed to have Father Colombo; he's been such a stepping stone in my faith. He's a spiritual leader and has played such an important role in how I've matured in years past.

One thing I've learned in the last few years, especially through Medjugorje, is that so many people focus on the divinity of Christ. They look at his miracles, like turning water into wine, healing people, and bringing people back from the dead. But as we can see from the Passion as a whole, especially the Garden of Gethsemane, he asked God the Father to take that cup away from him. He was afraid to go through what he was going to go through – that's where we see so much the human side of Jesus. You know, think of that fact that he actually walked on this earth like I am right now. Our Lord, our savior, He was born as a baby in the stable of muck, with lots of animals and dirt – that shows us that He came to earth as a person. We can't forget the meaning that Jesus came as a man. That's how I connect so much to the fact that He was a person, that allows me to have a connection with Him.

~*Christy, Ireland*

...I remember being in Arizona and we went go see Ivan speak at a church. I remember thinking how it could be that in this day and age there could be visionaries, like Saint Bernadette of Lourdes or the children at Fatima.

However, as life went on, life got busier and things became messier. Things happened in my immediate family and things started to breakdown and breakup. My kids, they went to Catholic school, but they started losing their faith. Then I started losing my faith. I thought how it could be that I say I am Christian but I'm never going to church, I'm never praying, I'm beginning to lose my children, and my husband has stopped going to Mass. I realize now that it wasn't the voice of God that was causing me these doubts.

Three years ago, I met a fellow nurse who told me about this doctor, Dr. Kathy Wolf. I learned she had been to Medjugorje, so I scheduled an appointment to see her! I told her I had read Mirjana's book, *My Heart Will Triumph*, and after reading it, I felt strongly called to come here to Medjugorje. I finally felt like there was hope. My life seemed empty, and although you could taste Medjugorje from home I felt that I really had to challenge myself and thought about how sick of being lukewarm I was. After talking to Kathy for an hour, she went to get me my robe to change into and brought me back a Medjugorje Rosary. There was something special there, a doctor is handing me a rosary that came from Medjugorje.

My friend Maria and I describe it here as a wrinkle in time between heaven and earth here. It's like you come to this place and so much resembles Jesus' time. The way people pray and support one another in prayer. Even the landscape is so simple like Christ's time. We say there is something different in the air here. I just have the sense that this place is ordained by God.

After a few days of being here, I realized it's not about the visionaries, it's all about God's presence wherever we are. Before my first time here, I hadn't been to confessions in 26 years...

~*Ann, USA*

I decided in June that I needed to come for some reason. I had heard stories from other people that have been, and I just felt the call to come here. My experience has been amazing. Completely amazing. The ambience of the place — the smells, the earthiness. It's real. It's all real here.

On Apparition Hill, all my friends were going up and I was hanging back because I'm afraid of heights. I can fly, but on the ground I'm afraid to climb. So, I struggled with the first few steps up, and everybody was ahead of me and I thought about turning around and coming back down.

And then I thought, "No, no, no. I need to go. I need to do this." But it was so scary.

I was just about to cry at every one of those stops. And then I got to the third Mystery of the Rosary, and I was listening to the commentary [by Medjugorje guide, Miki Musa] of the Mystery, and I thought, "Wow, I need to offer this up." Because I have two children that are out of the Church, and I want them back desperately, and I want Mary to bring them back. So I thought, "Okay, well let's just offer this up. This is a good penance to do."

So I offered it up, and the climb got easier. I was still scared, but it was easier.

When I got to the top, I'm standing there. I'm behind everybody still. We get to the Cross and the Virgin Mary, and I look up at the sun, and look away, then look back again. It's spinning and the colors were amazing. And that was my answer. I was supposed to do that climb. I'm so happy that I did it.

And I had an angel help me down. A young woman from Sicily walked up behind me and she said in broken English, "Give me hand." All the rest of the climb down, she held my hand and helped me. She was my guardian angel come to life.

~Darlene, USA

**Angeline:** [I've been to Medjugorje] four times. The first time, on my own at the age of twenty. The second time with my agnostic boyfriend who didn't believe at all, but after the fourth day, went for a hike on a mountain behind Mount Krisevac — the one with the radio tower on it — in the dark, got lost, and found God.

We then got married, he became a Catholic, and the third time we came back after we lost our first child. We went to Medjugorje and Assisi. We prayed for another child. After Assisi, after praying, through the intercession of Saint Francis and Saint Clare, I was pregnant and I had Clare. She got her name after Saint Clare.

**Clare:** This is my first time. I've found it really interesting. At the start, it was a lot to take in, especially with all the pilgrims. There're so many people here that it's hard to get a personal connection at the start, until you go and take some time by yourself and pray and reflect. By doing that, I have learned more about myself, and it's been a really good, interesting experience.

My favorite experience has been going up Apparition Hill, both for Ivan's apparition and going up with my mother — going up there and praying. It's so peaceful up there looking over Medjugorje and the statue of Mary. I just love it up there. We found a rock that we sit on underneath a tree. It's really peaceful there.

**Angeline:** She's claimed it as her rock. [...]

**Clare:** I definitely think this pilgrimage has increased my prayer life. I'm really excited to go home and talk to my younger siblings about it and to help them move towards the faith, if possible, both by my actions, and also, I bought them the rosary beads for the seven Our Father's, Hail Mary's, and Glory Be's. Because, as Mirjana said, Mary started [the visionaries] with that so I thought I'd help them learn that to start with. So, I'm really excited about that.

**Angeline:** I love hearing that from her. That's beautiful.

*~Clare & Angelina, Australia*

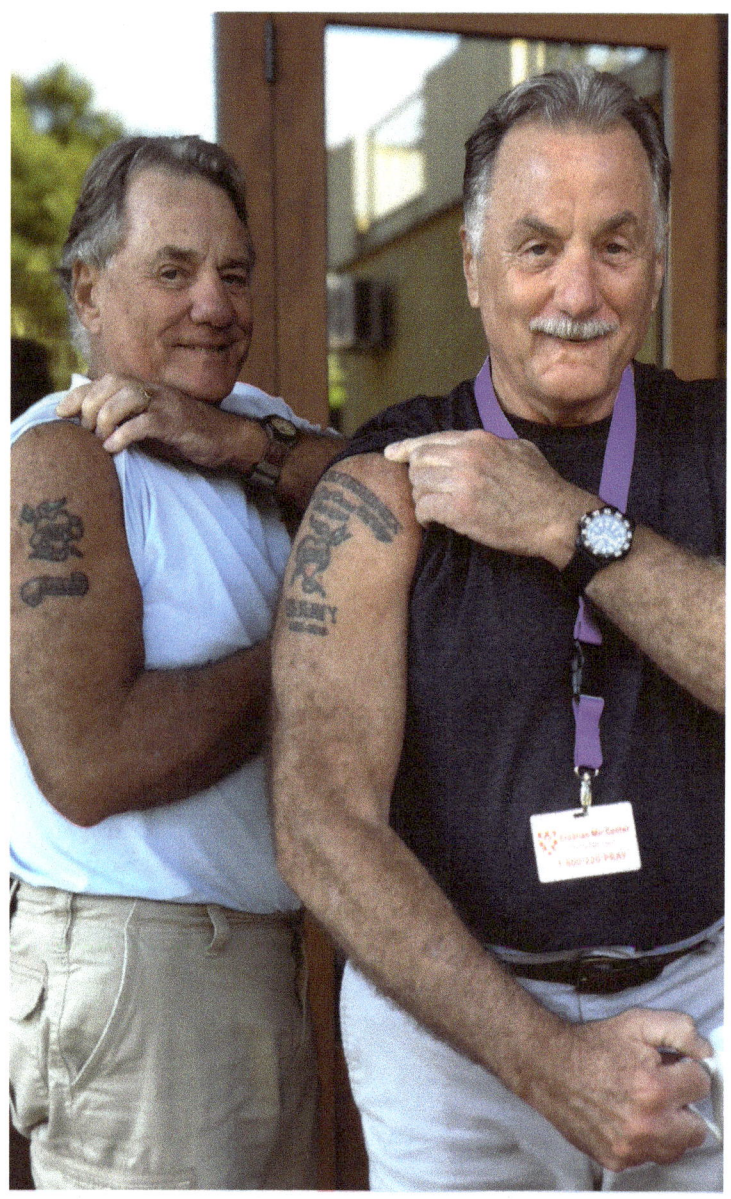

**Mike:** We've been best friends our whole life. We've shared all the things we've always done although we've been many miles apart around the world. Renee (my wife) and I were so moved and so blessed by our trip last year that we told my brother and sister-in-law and that's been our format most of our life. Especially since we've been married and our wives are close friends. Medjugorje is like the top of the mountain spiritually that we have experienced and that's been kind of exemplary for the relationship we've always had.

**Steve:** And I am not Catholic, and I never heard of Medjugorje until he came home last year and spoke so highly of it. I think being twins, I didn't have to talk much more about it. I said, "We are going." Kind of immediate credibility. If he thinks that much of it, we are on our way. It's kind of a twin thing. We are on the same frequency. We don't need to do a lot of qualifications or go down a check list. "Oh yeah, let's go."

**Mike:** Some twins go their whole life and are never close. Steve and I are the opposite. Everything but dressing alike... same tattoos.

"We won the trip through Stella Mar Pilgrimages three years ago, and [my son] Sawyer's finally healthy enough to get to come on this amazing pilgrimage. It's totally changed our life completely. I feel like we're all much closer as a family now. It's just been amazing. It's super peaceful. I didn't realize how at peace I needed to be until I came here. Sawyer's just been awesome. We've had an amazing week.

My whole family has had an amazing week. We're definitely gonna come back again and again. We can't wait to plan our next trip. We got to go to the apparition [of Our Lady to Mirjana on October 2nd]. I don't think I'll ever feel that way again in my life, until I get to go again, if I get to go, if the Blessed Mother calls us to come back up there.

But we also got to sit and talk to Mirjana, and her watching Sawyer was just so amazing. Honestly, it was so nice just seeing how she's just a normal mom.

Obviously, she's super special, but she just was normal and wanted to get to know Sawyer and get to know me. That was really unbelievable.

I think the coolest part, the night before the apparition, was walking back from town and hearing everyone pray and sing. That was just unbelievable. You could hear it from St. James Church."  ~*Catie, Florida USA*

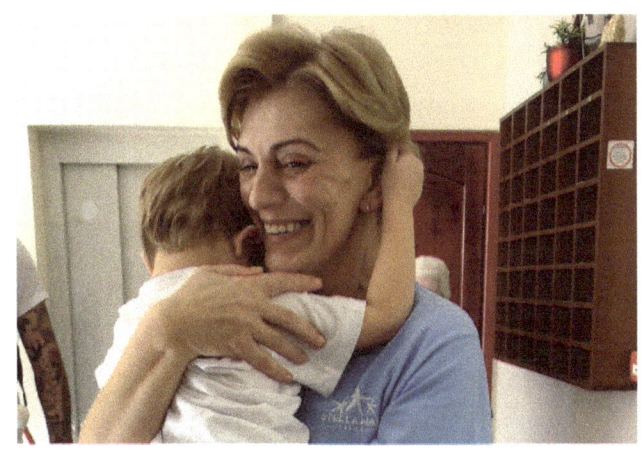

**Joanne:** The first time I came was in 1988. It was a lot different than it is now. There were no hotels, no roads, we walked everywhere through the fields, and there were tobacco fields here which there are not anymore. We stayed in people's homes. I came with my parents and my sister and my life changed. My life just changed immensely — my prayer life, my spiritual life. Then we got married a year later and I didn't come back [to Medjugorje] until 2015 with my friends. Joe didn't really want to come. It's our 30th anniversary so this is why he's here now.

So, I said, "It's our anniversary. What are we going to do? Where are we going to go?" And he's like, "Well where do you want to go?" And I said, "You know where I want to go." So he said, "Okay." And here we are together, finally, after thirty years.

**Joseph:** It's a very unique place. I'm a little taken aback by the number of people. Hearing the descriptions for the last almost thirty years, it was described as much quieter and peaceful. It's peaceful. You can get a lot of peace, but it's not a peaceful environment just with the sheer number of people.

So far, I've been pleasantly surprised and keeping an open heart and an open mind to what's to come. I hadn't been to confession in many, many years. The priest helped me through it a little bit which was nice. He was patient and told me to take my time and however long I needed to get it out. Probably before getting here it wouldn't have been my first choice for an anniversary trip, but now that I'm here, I'm glad I'm here[...]

**Joanne:** It's a whole different way of living your life — a whole different way of thinking, different way of praying. I love it here.

One of the fruits that I brought back from Medjugorje, I started in my church, every Wednesday night, we say the Rosary for peace [peace Rosary]. We do that every Wednesday night in our church. We've been doing it now for maybe ten years.

**Meghan:** We almost didn't come to Medjugorje together. We kind of worked it through that morning and said, "Okay, well then, we'll just kind of go as friends."

...This is the first time that I have ever felt like we've really been on the same page. Which, you can imagine being with someone for 25 years, what a huge gift that is, coming out of a weeklong trip. And he said something really profound here. He said, "You know, I realize you've kind of been carrying our family spiritually, and I'm ready to step up and be right there with you and to show our daughters that this what I believe too."

That is the gift of a lifetime to take home, because children follow what they see their parents doing, and while I have not, by any means, been a perfect role model, it does take a village. I think with the two of us united in our beliefs and in our faith and what we will do and show them, will make a huge impact going forward on our children and all those people that we love around us.

**David:** Getting up at 4 in the morning and going to Apparition Hill and waiting for Mirjana [for the apparition on May 2nd], it was 4 hours of hurry up and wait. And then once everything went silent, you're like, "Okay, this is what this is supposed to be." The only way I could describe it from my perspective was, it's almost like if I had anything negative in my body, call it negative juice, it just flew out of my body. This is what it's supposed to be, nice and calm and peaceful, and that's what it's been for me since we've been here.

**Meghan:** I don't feel worthy, but you know what, we are. That's why She's coming. So it's like, "Don't say that, Meghan. She wouldn't come if She didn't think we were worthy. He wouldn't send Her if He didn't think we were worthy." But it's very humbling. And then to have David here with me while going through all of this, it makes me feel like our marriage will be unstoppable now. That's a big gift. God has played a huge hand, prior to ever coming here, in the fact that we're still married. It's a miracle. We are blessed beyond words.

## OUR LADY'S MESSAGE TO MIRJANA ON NOVEMBER 2, 2019

"Dear children, my beloved Son always prayed and glorified the Heavenly Father. He always said everything to Him and trusted in His will. This is what you, my children, should also do, because the Heavenly Father always listens to His children. One heart in one heart – love, light and life.

The Heavenly Father gave Himself through a human face, and this face is the face of my Son. You, apostles of my love, you should always carry the face of my Son in your hearts and your thoughts. You should always think of His love and His sacrifice. You should pray to always feel His presence, because, apostles of my love, that is the way for you to help all those who do not know my Son, who have not come to know His love.

My children, read the book of the Gospel. It is always something new, it is what binds you to my Son who was born to bring the words of life to all of my children and to sacrifice Himself for all. Apostles of my love, carried by the love for my Son, bring love and peace to all of your brothers. Judge no one. Love everyone according to the love for my Son. In this way, you will also be caring for your soul, and it [your soul] is that what is most precious, which truly belongs to you. Thank you."

~Our Lady Queen of Peace, November 2

I've been here four times [...]

My family, they didn't really want me to come. In fact, they were getting a little adamant about it. But my determined nature, I just said, "Well, the more they say that, the more I'm going to do it, just to prove that a lady of 83 can do it with a bad back."

It's been such an adventure. It's sort of humbling because I actually do have to have people help me to a certain extent. So, you're sort of dependent, and I've never been like that. But it's humbling to know the goodness of people everywhere. I mean, somehow people would come up and say, "I'll take you up this ramp. I'll take care of your baggage. I'll sit with you." They bought me a Coke! It's just humbling. I cannot do everything that everyone's doing, but I don't care. Our Lady's here so it doesn't really matter.

The first time I came, we stayed in Mirjana's house. We were on the third floor. They had the second floor and the kitchen was down below. I came and I wanted to be by myself, but that's not God's plan. They didn't have enough separate rooms so there were three of us and two were young gals so I became kind of their dorm mother. They kept me up at night talking. Then the electricity went out. It was an experience. I felt for Mirjana and her family because they were living in the middle and we were tromping up and down. I don't know how she did it for all those years.

And then, in the morning, you'd look out the window and here's all these Italians and you can't get out. Mirjana goes out there and talks to them. Just so gracious, a very gracious person. Then, right after that, they finally stopped doing that and started building the hotel. I felt privileged that I was able to be in that group; that I could be in her home. But I did feel for them. I mean, how would you like to have people tromping in your house all year, and you're serving them food. I feel she's so very genuine. That's one of the things that got me. Just down to earth and very kind, a very nice person.

~Beverly, USA

**Tammy:** I think what made me want to camp out [before the apparition] was just to have a good spot; to be able to see Mirjana and experience it up close and personal.

**Allison:** This is 100% out of my comfort zone, but I was willing to do that just because I wanted to be as close to our Blessed Mother as possible so I could experience what she wanted to communicate to me.

**Tammy:** It was an experience. I would say it was fun, I was just so full of anticipation and excitement, I couldn't sleep. There was no way I could've slept. And I can't believe that I was awake for that long either, just sitting on those rocks.

**Allison:** And you met a lot of people. And it's funny how you kind of become like a little community with the people around you. Even meeting people that were connected to friends that have been here before. I just felt like the Holy Spirit was present in all of it and connecting in a special way or revealing even distress or evil going around. There was perspective in it to keep your focus on Our Lady and not to be distracted by all the distress.

**Tammy:** People were distracting. We knew what was coming when we were told about the screamers. The evil itself being present all around, it was kind of showing us our current world. It's everywhere. No matter what, it's everywhere, and if you take your eyes off of Jesus and Mary for a second, you'll lose it. The message might not come through for you.

**Allison:** [What inspired us to come was] watching *Apparition Hill*, reading Mirjana's book definitely gave me perspective, and then talking to friends that have been pilgrims before. They came in March. Watching the transformation in their life, complete transformation.

**Maryann:** I came almost three years ago, after my husband passed. I came to heal and to ... start my life. Then I went back home and I told Janet and she's been interested and we've been planning to go ever sense. There are a lot of others in my parish really anxious to hear back from us.

We are carrying so many prayers.

It's my second time here and it's Janet's first time. We heard we could camp out on the hill, so we just thought we would be able to get closer.

While we were sitting on the hill last night, we were remembering our friend whose daughter is struggling with mental illness, and another friend whose son is very ill. And the list just goes on and on of people who we are praying for. They were texting and saying "we need a miracle; we need a miracle." So, we were like we are going to be holding you in prayer tonight and we are with the Blessed Mother.

**Janet:** We were looking down on the Blue Cross so we thought we had a good spot. It was lovely because the musicians were playing. The music was lovely. We went up at 11:30 at night [the night before]. The anticipation was wonderful. At times you wonder if you're going to make it until the morning. It's amazing that you could snuggle down in those boulders and find a place.

**Maryann:** When the apparition happens, you can feel the presence of Our Lady and everyone's peaceful. I think I will always come back to that moment.

**Janet:** For sure. It is hard to describe. It's so fresh now. I am sure we will rehash it for a long time.

**Jesus Garcia:** I was 28 years old when I came to Medjugorje for the first time. I worked at the newspaper. My boss sent me out to write a news report. My colleague and I journeyed to Medjugorje and we returned totally changed. When we got back the news report became very important in Spain because it was the first time a high profile article was made about Medjugorje. It was 2006. After making that report, Gonzalo my colleague, who was 30 years old at the time, quit the newspaper company and became a seminarian. Today he is one of the happiest priests in Madrid and he still visits Medjugorje when he can. He became a priest and I did not.

Years later I began to write more articles and reports about Medjugorje. I wrote a book. It's a beautiful story. A girl read that book. Because of that book she came to Medjugorje, and in Medjugorje I met her, we got married, and had three kids. It's a story written by God.

**Borja:** Well here we are now making a documentary because we want Our Lady's message to reach the whole world. We are useless instruments but we know with God's grace and graces from Our Lady we want to help Her message to spread to more people. We have done it with books, videos, and now we want to do it on a larger scale. We gained experience making a movie about Lourdes and it's been beautiful to see Our Lady in the movie box office. You see Hell Boy, Tom Cruise, X-men, and then Our Lady! So we feel an obligation to share with the world the marvelous place we've come to know as Medjugurje.

*~Jesus & Borja, Spain*

I have been here 13 times. My first time was back in 1983. I went with the family that made the first film [Stanley and Marge Karminski]. They produced the first film on a tape. They had been praying and wanted a priest to go with them. I said, "Medji-what Medji-who...Medjugorje." And I agreed.

When I came here in '83, it was only other Croatian people. There were 8 in our group. The Franciscans had invited me to concelebrate the mass. Two of the visionaries took me by the hand and led me across the sanctuary to where they were seeing the Blessed Mother. Apparently, they heard the American priest was here and that was a novelty. That was about a year after the visions started. What was I thinking when I went into that room? I didn't know what was happening when I went in. Who were these girls? I didn't know who they were.

They didn't have a "V" on their forehead for "visionary." So, I went in and the room was full with Croatian people and they were all praying the Rosary. A crucifix on the wall. I just joined them praying the rosary. I had no idea the visitations would start right there. Then all of a sudden, they said the word for "She's here." They dropped down like a trap door opened up beneath them. That shook me up. Then it hit me. This must be where they see the Blessed Mother. I was watching them, each of the young ones. I saw Medjugorje at that time was just nothing. Literally dirt poor. No indoor plumbing near the church. I met Fr. Jozo and he brought me out to sit with the visionaries. It was still overwhelming to me. Word got out in my home area in New Jersey and Pennsylvania. "He's been to Medjugorje." I was a pastor of an inner-city church in Chester, Pennsylvania. Priests kept calling me if I could come talk to the people. I felt very uncomfortable with that because I didn't really understand it myself. I didn't know about the messages. I began to learn about that. Even in diners I went to, were overcrowded with people. I felt inadequate. I didn't know the whole story. But then I began to read about it and began to fill in the pieces. Through the years I would lead people here. 13 pilgrimages and here I am.   ~*Fr. John McFadden, USA*

**Michelle:** Fr. McFadden gave me the book [*My Heart Will Triumph*].

**Margaret:** I asked to read it. And she said, "sure" because I normally don't ask to read her books. I read it and I felt like I wanted to come. I felt like I was being called to come but I didn't think I'd ever come anytime soon. I thought maybe after I graduated college.

**Michelle:** She's like, "Hey Mom, so like how much does a trip to Medjugorje cost? Is that something I could ever do one day?" I said, "If Our Lady wants you there, she will get you there. My [other] daughter actually may be diagnosed with T-cell lymphoma. She's a young mom with three small children under the age of 5. The prognosis for that is not good. She's a nurse and as a mom, she could never go. Margaret said, "Why don't I go for her?" I told my mom what she said and my mom's like "Your granny just died and she had this money. She said I would know one day where to use that money. I'd like to send you both."

...I feel like I'll always come back. This place, it's home. It literally feels like my grandmother's house when I would go over there. She was Italian and she would say, "Can I get you something to eat?" And you would say, "No," and she'd say, "No, can I get you something to eat? Can I get you something to drink?" She would not stop until you took something. She was the reason we came to Medjugorje in the first place.

She passed away in 2014 and her death was so beautiful. We were all in the room, and the second they gave her the Last Rites, she opened her eyes really big and her eyes were glowing blue. Her eyes were brown... 5:15... I really, truly believe that the Blessed Mother came to get her.

She was a member of the Blue Army of Fatima. She always had stuff about Medjugorje so that's how we learned about it. After she died, I feel like when she got to Heaven, I think that she immediately started praying for all of the family.

I was the first one to come to Medjugorje. My sister came also on my second trip, but my entire family has seen graces upon graces poured out. We've gotten so much closer to the Rosary, so much closer to confession, and we've always been faithful Mass goers, but daily Mass has definitely been a big thing. And we also know we need to read the Bible more and try to do some type of fasting.

I decided to fast from alcohol for an entire year starting on the Anniversary — so June 24th/25th. Since I've started to do that, because I struggle with fasting on bread and water, so much grace has come. Because it is a sacrifice. When you're hanging out with your friends and they're all having fun and family things everyone's having a little bit of wine. I think that when you fast, when you give up something as a sacrifice, it leaves a space open for God to pour those blessings into your life and to pour those graces into your life. And He wants us, I think, to expect that when we give up something. So, it's been really beautiful.        ~*Aaron, Kansas USA*

**Anna:** This is my eighth or ninth trip to Medjugorje.

**Martha:** It'll be more for us. Ten or eleven. We get very excited. We like coming here. We try to come here every year. We come with the Mary's Meals group. Calum and Mariana are our grandparents and they came to Medjugorje…when did they come?

**Anna:** In the 1980s. '83 or '82.

**Martha:** And then they went back to Scotland and set up Craig Lodge which is a retreat place for pilgrims. They still come out here to Medjugorje quite a lot as well. Scotland is cold and wet and rainy, but it's nice. It's very green.

**Martha:** Adoration is my favorite part. I'm going to go to Adoration. I like that.

**Anna:** Getting ice cream!

**Bethany:** I like the evening Mass because it's big and there's loads of people.

**Tobi:** The heat's quite nice, coming from a cold country. And Adoration in the evening.

Back in 1983, when I was only fifteen years of age, my older sister read an article, a report that there were apparitions in Yugoslavia, as it was then, and we just decided to come — a bunch of teenagers. We came here just to try and find out more.

Medjugorje has impacted my life in so many different ways. That experience when I was a teenager really renewed my faith. And it had a huge impact on my wider family. It led my parents to turn our home into a Catholic retreat center. Then, out of this, this work of Mary's Meals grew which has become my life's work. And I met wife doing that work as well, so everything about my life, in some way, is connected to Medjugorje. I would encourage anyone to come to Medjugorje that hasn't come, whether they believe or not.

I'm not sure there's a lot to lose by coming here. There's certainly a huge amount to gain, and we see that in the lives of so many thousands of people around the world. That's something that fascinates me. I travel a lot to different countries, and so often I encounter beautiful works, beautiful projects, and so often you can trace them back to Medjugorje, to people whose lives have been changed here. So I really believe Medjugorje is changing the world in many different ways.

*I would encourage everyone just to come and experience it for yourself.*

~Magnus, Scotland

*Medj Note: Magnus is the founder of Mary's Meals, which feeds over 1.5 million children around the world.*

I'm involved in Cairos [prison ministry] at the California State Prison, a Level-4 maximum security prison. It's the most violent prison in the state. Up in Monroe, it was a medium security prison, so once guys proved they were lower risk and they were better behaved, they would go into that prison. This one, the security is much higher, everything is locked down, the men don't eat in a common area, they're fed in their cells, they're very, very angry, they're angry at themselves, and the Cairos Ministry really is designed for that. As I get closer to retirement, I'm thinking, "You know, sometimes I just don't feel like I'm getting through to these guys. Is there something better I should do? Something different I should do?" After I heard Mirjana speak, I'm like, "No, I'm in the right place." Because it's all about bringing the touch of Jesus Christ to those that have never felt it and those that have lost their faith.

So, I know I'm supposed to stay. [...] It's not about — this is what I always forget — it's not about me. It's not about me feeling good. It's not about being successful because we're not called to be successful, we're called to do the work that Christ has called us to. And I had kind of lost sight of that, I think. [...] I read Mirjana's book *My Heart Will Triumph*. I'm like, "Oh my gosh." Then I immediately went back and took my Fatima book, reread that. Then we did the *33 Days to Morning Glory*. My wife and I just did our consecration the other day.

What's neat about this is it's not a pilgrimage in the sense of the other pilgrimages that we've gone to. The Jesuits say, "You really need to build a personal relationship with Jesus Christ." This is all about building a personal relationship with Mary. My experience with this pilgrimage has been very similar to the Cairos four day retreat we do in prison. We bring these guys in, and they have got this look on their face like, "What is going on? What did I sign up for? What am I getting into?" And they're broken. And each day, we just see them grow and grow and grow and the last day, they're absolutely on fire. When I came here, I didn't really know what to expect, and each day, I just grew and grew and grew...
~*David, USA*

I first heard about Medjugorje back in 2000 from a friend who had gone through a conversion experience and had started giving materials on Medjugorje and Our Lady being here. He invited me to this Marian conference in Irvine, CA. I really enjoyed the conference and hearing about the conversion stories and miracles. I really felt called and inspired to go and I was in Medjugorje six weeks later. I was there on the Feast of the Immaculate Conception.

I experienced a deeper conversion in Medjugorje. I saw a lot of miracles and stuff like that but most importantly, there was a conversion of heart. When I got back to California, I felt God calling me to become a priest, and that is when I started discerning religious life. A few years later, I joined the Marian Fathers of the Immaculate Conception.

I've been to Medjugorje seven times now and every time it keeps building and building. I really encourage people to come here  you'll experience love and peace here like you never have before. The whole focus of Medjugorje is Our Lady leading us to Her son. It's all about Jesus. Often times people come here looking for some kind of sign or a miracle. What's important is to open your heart and mind to Our Lady. Don't focus too much on the secrets or the future but rather just open your heart to Our Lord.

~Fr. Angelo, USA

Mama Mary called me here October 1st, 1986 for the feast of Saint Therese of the Little Flower. So, I've been coming here a long time. I am Croatian.

I went to the mountain and I saw a big crowd on the left. It was German. Vicka was speaking to them, and I came to her so fast. I spoke German because I was in Germany for two years before I immigrated to America. I went to Vicka and I said, "I hope you live a thousand years." And she said, "Not thousand; hundred maybe."

So from that time, Father Petar at 9:30 came to the house. I went to confession with him, and I thought he remembered my confession. I'm a big sinner today, never mind then so many years ago, so I ran in my room. I didn't want to come out.

They called me a couple times and finally I said, "Mama Mary help me." So, I came out. He said, "Why are you so shy?" I said, "Father, I have to be honest with you. You are a priest. You represent Jesus. I think you remember all my sins." He said, "No. We don't remember." He told me to explain this to other people who fear to see the priest.

*Please come as soon as possible. The time is short. Your life is not gonna be the same. And if you think that you're not worth it, you probably are not, like I am not, but our Lord is not a liar. You are very important to the plan of salvation for the world.*

~Marija, Croatia

**Zoltan:** Our Lady used a very unusual way of bringing Julie back to the Church... Julie made a prayer to the Virgin Mary that she might one day meet John Taylor [base player for Duran Duran]...It took 32 years, but it was answered.

Then the next day, we came to Medjugorje. Julie was more favorably predisposed to things. We were here for the September 2nd vision in 2017.

**Julie:** The concert was just a few days before the apparition day.

**Zoltan:** The timing was perfect. So we went to Apparition Hill. It was a Saturday morning, and it was pretty full. We got there a few hours early and we could still go up and, we never saw Mirjana, but were within a few hundred feet of her. Just waiting and waiting and praying the Rosary, or at least I was. Julie, you describe your experienc

**Julie:** A few times over the years, I've been dabbling in other forms of Christianity. I was reflecting to myself that the last time I was in such a large group of people, of Christians, it was the more radical type. The speaking-in-tongues type. More of a circus show than anything else. Everybody trying to out-Christian the next person.

I'm looking around me, and everybody seems to be doing their own quiet thing, praying or crying quietly or some people were, like me, looking about, just observing. I started to wonder, "What am I supposed to be doing here? I know that I was brought here for a reason. Should I be praying? Should I be singing?"

Then I heard, both inside my head and outside, audibly, words of affirmation that whatever I bring to the table, that's what it should be. I'm not supposed to be like somebody else. Who I am, what I do, it's fine. It's okay. And I know that these words of affirmation came from Our Lady herself.

I'm not ready to reveal exactly the words that were said to me, but it was said in a way that it could only be for me. Almost like a private joke. It couldn't be for the people around me or the person next to me. This was mine. And because it was so personal, I almost started laughing. It was almost very much like a private joke, but I stayed quiet. I didn't want to bother the people around me, because they were doing their own thing. I've got my thing. They have their thing.

**Zoltan:** This was during the silence of when the apparition was happening.

**Julie:** It was about a half a year later…I made peace with the Church without actually being Catholic. Taking all these little steps forward and little steps forward knowing that there was a threshold to cross before becoming Catholic, and it just occurred to me that I've hit that threshold already. It's somewhere behind me. I don't know when I went over it. But yeah, I think I'm back home now.

[…] I know that some people would be put off at the idea that Our Lady would use a secular band to draw somebody to the Church. To me, it's further proof that God can use whatever he freaking wants as a tool to draw people to the Cross.

**Zoltan:** If you think about the story of Our Lady of Guadalupe, and it's not like our story is anywhere near as significant, I don't want to sound grandiose, but what did Mary do with Guadalupe? She used the Aztec imagery, their language, to communicate with them. I'm sure for some of the Europeans, that might have felt like, "Well, why is She using pagan symbolism to speak to these people?" Because that was their language. She used what spoke to them, and was able to convey the message of Christ through their own imagery. And in a way, Mary used a secular thing, decidedly not a Catholic band, but She used something that Julie knew and broke into her heart.

**Julie:** And because of that, this necklace that I have, I use a medal, Our Lady of Guadalupe because of Her use of language to speak to whoever She's directly speaking to, and a Duran Duran pendant because that is how She spoke to me. She spoke my language.

## OUR LADY'S MESSAGE TO MIRJANA ON DECEMBER 2, 2019

"Dear children, As I am looking at you who love my Son, my heart is being filled with tenderness. I am blessing you with a motherly blessing. With a motherly blessing, I am also blessing your shepherds– you who speak the words of my Son, who bless with His hands and who love Him so much that you are ready to make every sacrifice for Him with joy. You are following Him, who was the first shepherd, the first missionary.

My children, apostles of my love, to live and work for others, for all those whom you love through my Son, is the joy and comfort of earthly life. If through prayer, love and sacrifice the Kingdom of God is in your hearts, then your life is joyful and bright. Among those who love my Son and who love each other through Him, words are not necessary. A gaze is sufficient for the unspoken words and unexpressed feelings to be heard. There where love reigns, time no longer counts. We are with you.

My Son knows you and loves you. Love is that which brings you to me and through that love I will come to you and speak to you of the works of salvation. I desire for all of my children to have faith and to feel my motherly love which leads them to Jesus. Therefore, you, my children, wherever you go, illuminate with love and faith as apostles of love. Thank you."

~Our Lady Queen of Peace, December 2

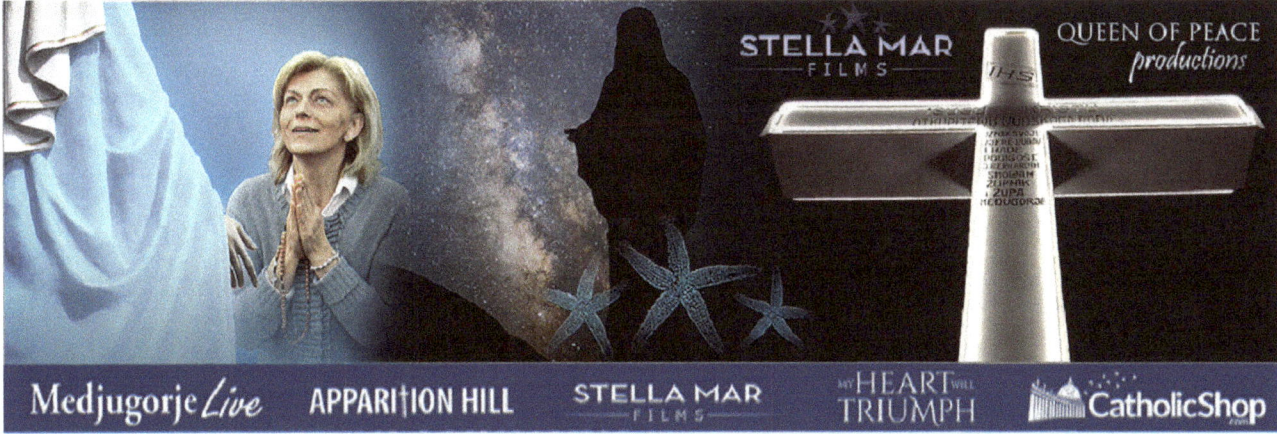

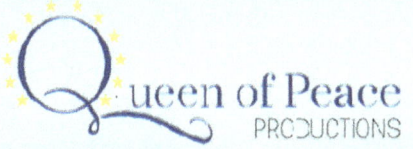

STELLA MAR
FILMS
QUEEN OF PEACE
productions
Medjugorje Live
APPARITION HILL
STELLA MAR
FILMS
MY HEART WILL
TRIUMPH
CatholicShop

Queen of Peace
PRODUCTIONS

Queen of Peace Productions is a non-profit organization dedicated to spreading the messages of Medjugorje, especially to "those yet to know God's love." We rely on your support to continue our mission and increase our reach in the world. Please consider making a tax-free donation to: *Queen of Peace Productions; 317 Riveredge Blvd, Suite 102; Cocoa, FL 32922.* Learn more at ***qopproductions.org.***

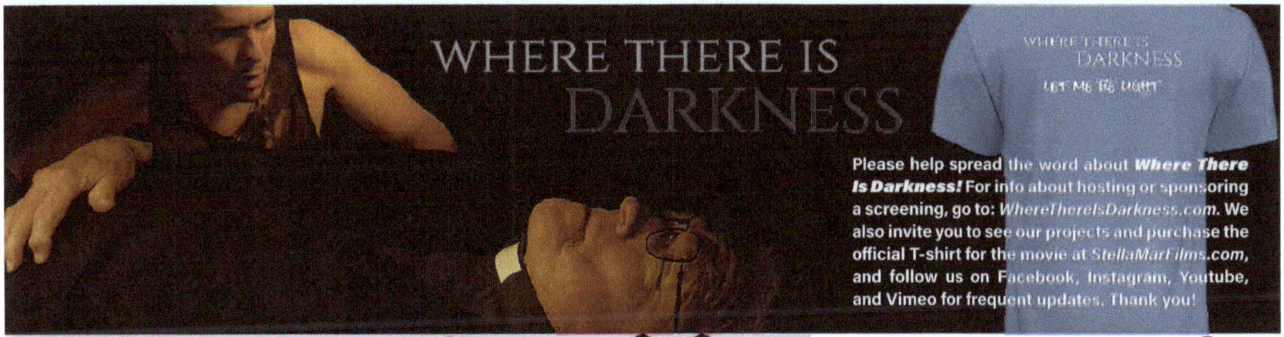
WHERE THERE IS
DARKNESS
Please help spread the word about ***Where There Is Darkness!*** For info about hosting or sponsoring a screening, go to: *WhereThereIsDarkness.com.* We also invite you to see our projects and purchase the official T-shirt for the movie at *StellaMarFilms.com*, and follow us on Facebook, Instagram, Youtube, and Vimeo for frequent updates. Thank you!

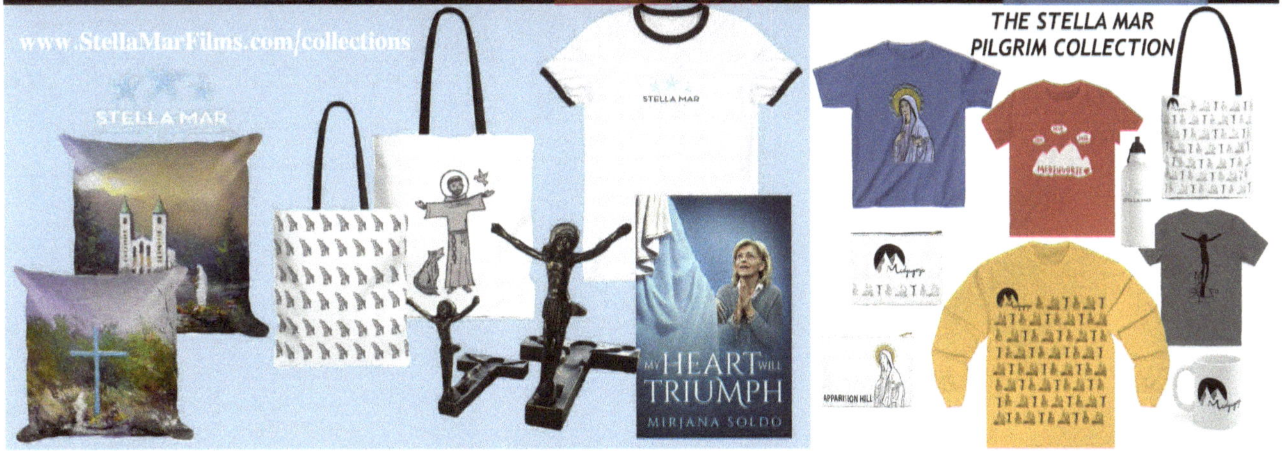
www.StellaMarFilms.com/collections
STELLA MAR
THE STELLA MAR
PILGRIM COLLECTION
MY HEART WILL
TRIUMPH
MIRJANA SOLDO
APPARITION HILL